A Nonfiction Book by Cy Kellett

A TEACHER OF STRANGE THINGS

Who Jesus Was, What He Taught,
& Why People Still Follow Him

Catholic
Answers
Press

Published by Catholic Answers, Inc.
2020 Gillespie Way
El Cajon, California 92020
1-844-239-4952 (toll-free) orders
619-387-0042 fax
catholic.com

Printed in the United States of America
Cover by Theodore Schluenderfritz
Interior by Russell Graphic Design

978-1-68357-228-2
978-1-68357-229-9 Kindle
978-1-68357-230-5 ePub

For Missy, who else?

"See what love the Father has given us, that we should be called children of God; and so we are" (1 John 3:1).

CONTENTS

PART TWO

What Jesus Taught

PART THREE

Why People Still Follow Jesus

With gratitude to my parents, Jo Anne and Cyril, for my life, for my six brothers and sisters, and, more than I can ever say, for handing on to me the Faith as they received it, in the one Lord, Jesus, who makes all things new.

"Everyone who believes that Jesus is the Christ is a child of God, and everyone who loves the parent loves the child. By this we know that we love the children of God, when we love God and obey his commandments. For this is the love of God, that we keep his commandments. And his commandments are not burdensome. For whatever is born of God overcomes the world; and this is the victory that overcomes the world, our faith. Who is it that overcomes the world but he who believes that Jesus is the Son of God?" (1 John 5:2–5).

INTRODUCTION

Modern life includes this strange reality—in the midst of it are millions of people who claim that they have a personal relationship with a man who died 2,000 years ago.

These people are treated as a normal part of the world. They are acceptable as movie stars, politicians, schoolteachers, doctors, and so on.

In courts of law, their testimony is considered as reliable as anyone else's.

And yet they say that this ancient man, Jesus, was raised from the dead, is still alive (is, in fact, alive forever), and is their friend.

We can see why this sometimes drives atheists and secularists to exasperation. They must ask themselves, "Am I the only one bothered by this? Doesn't anyone else see how weird it is that all around us are people who claim to know a dead man of the ancient world?"

Certainly, part of the reason that this claim of friendship with Jesus is acceptable even in the modern world is that it is not a new thing. People tend to be respectful of things that have been around for a long time. And, what is more, even the secular person has to admit that Christians generally behave themselves. For the most part, they contribute to civic life and go along with progress.

They are only dangerous (to the secularist way of thinking) when they get in the way of progress. In the eighteenth century, for instance, the complaint was that Christians got in the way of political revolutions. In the early twentieth century, the complaint was that they got in the way of economic—especially socialist—revolutions. More recently, especially with the broad acceptance of evolutionary biology and with medical innovations in birth control, abortion, and embryonic research, the complaint has been that Christians get in the way of science.

Still, for the most part, Christians don't go out of their way to make trouble, and, because their beliefs are ancient, they get a pass when it comes to their head-scratching ideas about Jesus.

I suspect that it's also the case that, recently, secularists have comforted themselves with the notion that belief in Jesus is on its way out. This strange situation—a modern world filled with so many people who cling to the pre-modern claim that Jesus is alive—can't go on forever.

To some extent, they have been right. A good portion of the world has undergone or is undergoing a process of de-Christianizing. But even this de-Christianizing hasn't entirely done the trick. Every day, new people are claiming that Jesus lives and that they know him, and in some places where de-Christianizing had looked quite successful, there are signs of *re*-Christianizing.

And wherever people claim to have met Jesus, they also report that their life has become more contented and more peaceful. They are *happier.*

No, life as a follower of Jesus does not suddenly lose its frustrations, nor do evils disappear, but even amid the hurts and wrongs of the world a new thing becomes present in the follower of Jesus, at least if their testimony is to be believed. This new thing lightens hearts and opens new possibilities.

To the propagandists of the modern world, this happiness must be a great lie or at least a delusion, and so they caricature Christian joy as if Christians were actually secretly creepy or twisted. Likewise, the real history of Christian culture is often distorted by those who cannot accept that followers of Jesus are really as happy and at peace as they claim. They exaggerate the violence and venality of Christian society and excuse the far harsher violence and venality of pre-Christian society in order to deny a reality that is obvious to any sane person: in countless families and tribes, nations and cultures, wherever the story of Jesus took root, a new element appeared in the alloy of culture, giving it new potentials.

This, too, is part of the strangeness of the story of Jesus. Wherever it takes root, society becomes manifestly less violent, more educated, and generally happier; but somehow the world spends a lot of time saying the opposite. It is almost as if there were a spirit loose in this world of resistance to Jesus.

But even in a society, like ours, that refuses to recognize its own history, the name of Jesus does not fade. Even as our society reduces Christianity to a marginal role, the story of Jesus risen from the dead is still shared, and people continue to claim that they have met him, that he has changed their lives, and that he is their friend.

You simply cannot claim to be an open-minded and rational adult without, at least once, giving this strange reality fair consideration.

Likewise: given the claims made about Jesus, his extraordinary teachings, and his towering place in world history, a reasonable adult really can't go through life without giving these things open-minded consideration, at least once.

Yet many try. Why?

Part of the reason may be that there is so much emotion and cultural strife surrounding him. Even those who develop an interest in finding out about Jesus might remain silent about their interest in order to protect themselves from the avalanche of other people's feelings and opinions that will surely fall on them if they ask even the smallest question about Jesus.

There is something reasonable about this. Modern society is constantly being swept by fads and movements, which is tiring. The person who does not jump at every claim is often the most prudent.

But Jesus is not one of those fads or movements. He far predates all of that, and his influence has persisted for so long that it calls upon us to overcome our reluctance and think the whole thing through, as I said, at least once. The Jesus phenomenon is strange in its origins and in its consequences.

Whatever happened in Judea around the year 30, it is utterly unique. Nothing like it has happened before or since.

And although we can also see plainly that Christians have become corrupt again and again, and that the name of Jesus has been abused by preachers, politicians, and prudes, the allure of the man himself (and of the saints, artists, thinkers, and ordinary people whom he inspired) presses each of us for a response.

His claims about himself call for an answer. *Who is this?*

His transformative place in history also calls for an answer. *Should I follow him or reject him?*

This book is organized around a simple proposition: now is the best time to consider these questions and decide for ourselves.

With that goal in mind, my intention is to share the facts about Jesus as most Christians throughout most of history, including today, understand them. I hope to do so in a way that is accessible to any person of good will. Most especially, I will try, though I am a follower of Jesus, not to present him in a manipulative or propagandistic way.

In my view, the truth about him is enough, and it is so consistent with human flourishing that it is best just to present it without embellishment or salesmanship. My hope is to present it as I have received it because, for me, it has met every test of reason while also surpassing all my expectations for bringing happiness.

It is not so complicated, this task of presenting Jesus. He taught in a very accessible way. His story is straightforward. Yet it also has a poetry and a beauty that can, like all good stories, refresh the mind and enliven the heart with each retelling.

From him, though he spoke in a very simple manner, layer after layer of insight emerges, so that even the most brilliant minds can spend a lifetime exploring his meaning. So we cannot uncover all those layers in this little book, but we do not need to. He called his teaching "the good news of the kingdom of God" (Luke 4:43). And, as one of my teachers used to say, "It's not really good news if you need a college degree to understand it."

Still, although the basic teaching of Jesus is easy to understand, it is not always easy to accept because to accept what Jesus teaches is to step into an alarming world.

His is a world in which angels and demons have everyday dealings with humans; in which common items such as a drop of water or a crust of bread can be filled with powers greater than a thousand suns. His is a world in which human choices *matter*, not just for the moment, but for eternity.

Without question, the Jesus story is reasonable—it can pass every test of the historian, the philosopher, and the scientist. And it is accessible to any person who wants to grasp it. But to grasp it involves accepting truths that are far beyond what our modern minds usually will entertain.

He is a teacher of strange things, a doer of strange deeds, a man of strange manners; and listening to him raises questions that go to the very core of our existence—and our destiny.

PART ONE

WHO JESUS WAS

1

Suddenly,
a Public Life

At about thirty years old, Jesus began life as a public figure. His entry into public life appears to have been sudden and shocking. From their reactions, it seems that those who knew him had seen few, if any, signs of his intentions or of his extraordinary abilities.

In the early days of his public life, some members of his family evidently got reports that he was "beside himself" (Mark 3:21). (Some translations go so far as to say he seemed "out of his mind.") At one point in his public ministry, he visited his hometown, and the people there "were astonished, and said, 'Where did this man get this wisdom and these mighty works? Is not this the carpenter's son?'" (Matt. 13:54–5).

The earliest biography of Jesus was written by a man we know as Mark, who was a follower of Peter the apostle. Mark gives a sense, almost certainly based on the memories of Peter, of what those first days were like as Jesus began his public life:

In those days Jesus came from Nazareth of Galilee and was baptized by John in the Jordan. And when he came up out of the water, immediately he saw the heavens opened and the Spirit descending upon him like a dove; and a voice came from heaven, "Thou art my beloved Son; with thee I am well pleased." The Spirit immediately drove him out into the wilderness. And he was in the wilderness forty days, tempted by Satan; and he was with the wild beasts; and the angels ministered to him.

Now after John was arrested, Jesus came into Galilee, preaching the gospel of God, and saying, "The time is fulfilled, and the kingdom of God is at hand; repent, and believe in the gospel." And passing along by the Sea of Galilee, he saw Simon and Andrew the brother of Simon casting a net in the sea; for they were fishermen. And Jesus said to them, "Follow me and I will make you become fishers of men." And immediately they left their nets and followed him.

And going on a little farther, he saw James the son of Zeb'edee and John his brother, who were in their boat mending the nets. And immediately he called them; and they left their father Zeb'edee in the boat with the hired servants, and followed him. And they went into Caper'na-um; and immediately on the sabbath he entered the synagogue and taught. And they were astonished at his teaching, for he taught them as one who had authority, and not as the scribes. And immediately there was in their synagogue a man with an unclean spirit; and he cried out, "What have you to do with us, Jesus of Nazareth? Have you come to destroy us? I know who you are, the Holy One of God."

But Jesus rebuked him, saying, "Be silent, and come out of him!" And the unclean spirit, convulsing him and crying with a loud voice, came out of him. And they were all amazed, so that they questioned among themselves, saying, "What is this? A new teaching! With authority he commands even the unclean spirits, and they obey him." And at once his fame spread everywhere throughout all the surrounding region of Galilee.

And immediately he left the synagogue, and entered the house of Simon and Andrew, with James and John. Now Simon's mother-in-law lay sick with a fever, and immediately they told him of her. And he came and took her by the hand and lifted her up, and the fever left her; and she served them. That evening, at sundown, they brought to him all who were sick or possessed with demons. And the whole city was gathered together about the door. And he healed many who were sick with various diseases, and cast out many demons; and he would not permit the demons to speak, because they knew him.

And in the morning, a great while before day, he rose and went out to a lonely place, and there he prayed. And Simon and those who were with him followed him, and they found him and said to him, "Everyone is searching for you." And he said to them, "Let us go on to the next towns, that I may preach there also; for that is why I came out." And he went throughout all Galilee, preaching in their synagogues and casting out demons" (Mark 1:9–39).

Mark shows the entry of Jesus into public life as a dramatic break with everyday reality in which all were "amazed." Quite suddenly, something exciting is happening. With Jesus, a new reality is present, full of power and mystery.

Notice here that this new public ministry of Jesus has him operating on three different levels; or, if you will, that he is in relationship with three different realms: the *realm of spirits*, the *everyday world*, and a *new community* he chooses for himself from out of the world.

First, the relationship with God and the spiritual world is shown in the baptism, the voice of God, the satanic temptations, and the angels.

Second, the relationship with the whole human world is shown in his mission to heal people and in his call to all people to repent and believe in the kingdom of God.

And finally, his relationship with a small group of specially chosen students is shown in his call of Simon, Andrew, James, and John. (Later, this group will grow and become what Jesus calls by a word that in Greek means "those who are called out"; in English it is rendered by the word *church*.)

These three levels of relationships are all part of one effort on the part of Jesus, and with his very first public words he says what that effort is when he tells people that the *kingdom of God* is at hand. He is bringing that new thing into being. The spiritual world and the human world are to be wrapped up in this new thing that is happening: the dawning of the kingdom of God.

The ministry of Jesus, therefore, bridges the human and the divine. At his baptism, when the heavens are torn open, we are to understand that heaven and earth are no longer to be separate realms but are to be joined—because this person, Jesus, is somehow able to bring them together.

But the call of the apostles makes something else clear from the beginning: he is not going to do his work alone. He also intends to establish an institution that can continue to act as that connection between heaven and earth after he has finished his earthly mission. Thus Jesus can extend the effects of his work over time to the whole world, so that the kingdom of God—that mysterious joining of the human and the divine—can be made real everywhere, for everyone, and forever.

It is no accident that the very first Gospel portrays Jesus, from the start of his public life, as working on these three levels. We are meant to see him as operating authoritatively both in the world of spirits and in the world of humans, but not doing so as a loner. Though he and his work are absolutely unique, he chooses to involve others in his work by calling people—a Church—to cooperate with him in uniting the divine and the human.

All four Gospels also make clear that *Peter* plays a central role in the Church that Jesus founds. He is mentioned in the Gospels more than all the other disciples combined, and, in story after story, his special role is emphasized. To be sure, the public work of Jesus starts before he calls Peter, and it far exceeds what Peter comprehends. But Jesus chooses to put Peter and the other disciples right next to him throughout his public years.

And what Peter witnesses immediately upon becoming a follower of Jesus is shocking: an unknown thirty-year-old, from a tiny little town not far from where Peter himself grew up, comes teaching with power and authority and performs miracles—freeing people from demons and healing the sick.

If the borderland between heaven and earth is the "where" of Jesus' ministry, we see right from the beginning three key components that make up the "what" of his ministry, the three actions he takes as the one who brings heaven and earth together: he teaches the kingdom of God, he casts out demons, and he heals the sick.

If we reflect on Christianity across the centuries, we can note that it has not only remained on the same terrain— acting as a meeting place for the divine and the human—but has carried on the same mission. The Church invented the university, the hospital, and the local parish, for instance, in order to perpetuate Jesus' work by teaching, healing, and making holy. This is the Christian life because the Christian life is modeled on Jesus.

The news that Jesus was able to teach and heal and cast out demons spread like fire, and in the early days of his public life he was received with an outpouring of joy. Matthew's Gospel describes these wild early days this way:

His fame spread throughout all Syria, and they brought him all the sick, those afflicted with various diseases and pains, demoniacs, epileptics, and paralytics, and he healed them. And great crowds followed him from Galilee and the Decap'olis and Jerusalem and Judea and from beyond the Jordan (Matt. 4:24–25).

For weeks, for months, for years, Peter and the other disciples took all this in as they followed along; at one point, exclaiming to one another, "What sort of man is this?" (Matt. 8:27).

This is the question we will try to answer first.

2

His World

Jesus was born sometime between 2 and 6 B.C., during the reign of Caesar Augustus.

Augustus was one of the greatest military and political leaders in the history of the world and was called "the son of a god" because he had been adopted by Julius Caesar, whom the Roman Senate had declared a god. However, he far exceeded Julius Caesar in his accomplishments, growing and strengthening the Roman Empire and creating institutions for it that would make it stable and prosperous for hundreds of years.

The rule of Augustus began a period called the *Pax Romana*, more than 200 years of relative peace throughout the Roman world. The fact that Jesus was born just at the beginning of this long period of peace and safety would play an important part in the spread of the religion that he founded.

Jesus grew up in a small town at the northern end of the traditional Jewish homeland of Israel, about 1,400 miles to the east of Rome, near the eastern edge of the empire. At one time, Israel had been an independent kingdom, but by the time Jesus was born, for several generations Israel had been ruled either by Romans or by leaders assigned by the Romans.

Three cultures dominated that part of the world: Jewish, Greek, and Roman.

The Jewish culture into which Jesus was born was more than 1,500 years old. The Romans respected it because of its great age, but it was very different from Roman culture. In fact, the Jews were unlike any other group in the Roman world. They did not worship many gods but only one God, the creator of everything, and they believed that God was not aloof to the fortunes of the world, like the gods of the ancient world who were mostly interested in themselves, but was deeply concerned with justice and mercy.

Their understanding of God's concern for justice and mercy, and their experience of him as holy, gave the Jews the impetus to live by a strict moral code, one that made them stand out as somewhat strange among their neighbors.

The Jews, in fact, considered it their role to stand out. They had a history of prophets who spoke to them about God, and these prophets made them understand that God had called them to reveal to the world the reality of the one God who calls *all* people to justice and mercy.

By the time of the birth of Jesus, Jewish culture had spread around the Roman world, where it attracted millions of followers and admirers, both Jewish and gentile. It had also extended beyond the Roman world into places as far away as Persia, and possibly even into India and Ethiopia.

This Jewish culture was centered around the temple in Jerusalem, where Jewish priests offered animal sacrifices, and around local synagogues where people met to study and pray. Like the *Pax Romana*, Judaism's vast international network of synagogues would be vital to the spread of the religion Jesus founded.

The *Greek* culture was almost as important as the Jewish culture in the area of Jesus' birth. Greeks, under the leadership of Alexander the Great, had conquered Israel, Egypt, and all of Asia as far away as India more than 300 years before Jesus. These Greeks had brought their language, their philosophy, and their love of beauty and reason with them wherever they went.

In a sense, they were the first globalizers. They wanted to draw the whole world into the Greek way of doing things. This caused friction with many local cultures, including the local culture of the Jews. Nonetheless, the Christian scriptures would be written entirely in Greek, and Greek language and philosophy became essential to the later spread of the religion Jesus founded.

Finally, the land where Jesus lived was influenced by its rulers, the *Romans*. They admired the Greeks, sent their children to Greek schools, and imitated them in many ways, but they were far better at government than the Greeks had ever been. Their rule was often violent, but they used violence for a purpose—to keep things running smoothly. Until modern systems were developed, the Romans were the best ever at keeping vast networks of people and trade running smoothly.

When we read about the life of Jesus in the books and letters written by his followers, we see evidence everywhere of a world that was flourishing because of the rich inputs of these various cultures. But we also see a world that was full of tension because of frictions between these cultures.

The town of Nazareth, where Jesus grew up, was a very small and traditional Jewish town, but just four miles away there was a larger town called Sepphoris. This larger town, though mostly Jewish in population, was Greek in its manner of life.

Jesus almost certainly knew Sepphoris well. He might even have worked there as a carpenter. He would have been well acquainted with its multilingual and multicultural setting. This diverse reality—with its many gifts and many tensions—was a fact of life that everyone in Jesus' part of the world had to navigate.

In many ways, his world was like ours. It had a relatively stable international system and a highly functioning civil structure, and it was well organized and interconnected. Its solidity is demonstrated by the fact that the last emperor in the western part of the empire would not be deposed until almost 500 years after Jesus, and the eastern part of the empire would go on, in one way or another, for more than a thousand years.

In addition to the social and political facts of life in his world, however, the geography of his homeland also played an important part in the spread of the religion that Jesus founded.

He lived his entire life at the point where Africa, Asia, and Europe come together, and his message was carried deep into those continents within a few years of his death. We know from the Acts of the Apostles that at least one person carried news of Jesus to Ethiopia within about ten years of his death (Acts 8:26–40). His own twelve apostles seem to have made it as far as India in the east and Spain in the west before they died. Even as far away as the British Isles he had worshippers almost certainly by the early to mid 100s.

Thus, within a few hundred years, the religion taught by Jesus united tens of millions of Africans, Asians, and Europeans into a new kind of society—a non-governmental, multi-cultural, multi-lingual society held together by shared belief in Jesus as Lord.

3

A Crisis of Identity

We know about Jesus because the people who remembered him left a historical record. We have biographies of him from four different writers, all finished within seventy years of his life. No other ancient person—not even Julius Caesar—has biographies written so close to the time of his own life and with such an ancient and voluminous chain of manuscripts. We have more first-hand and second-hand knowledge of Jesus from writings that we know have been preserved faithfully across the centuries than we do about any other ancient figure.

Despite all of this, the modern person who would like the facts about Jesus faces a serious problem, and that problem starts with Jesus himself.

He claimed to be God. Or, to put it more specifically, he claimed to be the God of the Jews: the one God, creator and lord of everything.

There is no evidence at all that this claim was invented by his followers or biographers after the fact. There is no evidence, either, that what he meant was something like, "I am God. You are God. We are all God."

No. He claimed to be unique, to be a man unlike you and me, the one and only God. And not only did he claim this identity, he made this claim the central point of his public life. In many ways, his claims about his own identity overshadow everything else he said and did.

He was sent to his execution for the crime of claiming to be God, and the main witness against him was himself. We find the earliest narrative of his trial in the Gospel of Mark. Jews do not name God—they use euphemisms to identify him—so at the trial Jesus is asked whether he is the son of "the Blessed."

And Jesus replies using the words *I am*.

Just saying "yes" would have been scandalous, of course, but what makes this admission particularly shocking is that in the most sacred Jewish texts, "I am" is the name *God gives himself* (Exod. 3:14).

Here is what Mark writes:

Now the chief priests and the whole council sought testimony against Jesus to put him to death; but they found none. For many bore false witness against him, and their witness did not agree. And some stood up and bore false witness against him, saying, "We heard him say, 'I will destroy this temple that is made with hands, and in three days I will build another, not made with hands.'" Yet not even so did their testimony agree.

And the high priest stood up in the midst, and asked Jesus, "Have you no answer to make? What is it that these men testify against you?" But he was silent and made no answer. Again the high priest asked him, "Are you the Christ, the Son of the Blessed?" And Jesus said, "I am; and you will see the Son of man sitting at the right hand of Power, and coming with the clouds of heaven." And the high priest tore his mantle, and said, "Why do we still need witnesses? You have heard his blasphemy. What is your decision?" And they all condemned him as deserving death (Mark 14:55–64).

Jesus' condemnation and death, we can see here, are a direct result of his own identity claims. He is killed for claiming to be God. By making these claims and sticking with them even unto death, Jesus cuts off the possibility that any honest recounting of his biography could leave those parts out while presenting him as merely a good man. His story is either the story of one who made false claims, or it is the story of God.

This strange question of identity sets Jesus apart from other historical figures, even other great religious figures. Mohammed, Buddha, Moses, and all the other religious founders are men who came to an enlightened insight or claimed to receive a divine call. Their identity is not the central question about them—their wisdom is, or the revelation God made to them, or their ability to lead.

Not so with Jesus. With him, identity is the whole game. On this question he rests all his credibility. He knew full well that his claims created a crisis for the people who met him and for his society as it struggled with the passions aroused by his claims—passions that swamped him, ended his earthly ministry, and brought about his death.

Everything else we know about him, as a kind healer and a teacher of peace and forgiveness, must be seen in light of the question of his identity. His claim to be God disrupts the normal functioning of his society, and it disrupts any normal attempt to study him as a normal historical figure. (And this disruption is part of his mission, too.)

His accusers and killers are not merely mean people who can't deal with a kind and forgiving rabbi. Rather, they can't deal with the disruption caused by his identity claim. They have to shut down the question of his identity, put it and him to death once and for all in order to preserve the peace.

This presentation of himself as divine is so important to Jesus that even as he was being questioned by the man who would put him to death, Jesus' primary concern was whether Pontius Pilate had begun to guess at his true identity.

"Are you the king of the Jews?" (John 18:33), Pilate asks, and Jesus, rather than answer with a simple yes or no, probes Pilate to see if he might find within this powerful Roman any inkling of a sincere desire to know.

"Do you say this of your own accord, or did others say it to you about me?" (John 18:34).

In other words, *Now that you have met me, are you wondering about me, are you sensing something mysterious about me, or are you just looking for evidence to convict me?*

This was not outrageous hope on Jesus' part. Earlier in his ministry, at least one high-ranking Roman official had accepted his claims (Luke 7:1–10). So, in this moment, rather than fighting for his life or defending himself against a charge of rebellion, Jesus looks for signs that Pilate—the one who seems to hold all the power—might be onto something strange about Jesus, something that will open Pilate to hear what Jesus has to say.

Those who wrote his earliest biographies—the writers of the Gospels—did not pretend to be neutral about Jesus. They accepted his claim to be God. They considered themselves to be writing the biography of the one man in all of history who was a divine person.

This leaves the modern reader with a challenge. How do we make sense of these writings?

We can accept them as faithfully handed on by those who knew him. But in that case, we have to accept his claims. If we decide at the outset that we can't accept his claims, as we read his biographies we have to mentally adjust their contents to make them fit our presupposition that he is not God. We have to modernize his story or spiritualize it or turn it into an allegory or myth in order to extract what we think is the real story hidden within.

The modern person, then, who wants to get "just the facts" of who Jesus was, cannot do so without making a preliminary choice—to accept the claims his biographers make about him, or to reject them and piece together some alternate version of the story.

4

Modern Attempts to Make Sense of Jesus

Was Jesus God? Did he really do miracles? Can we accept what his friends said about him? Did he rise from the dead?

The modern person who wants to answer these hard questions is confronted with three facts that need an explanation:

Fact one: He was a real person born in the Roman Empire during the reign of Augustus.

Fact two: Widespread accounts describing him as the self-proclaimed Son of God, a miracle worker who rose from the dead, can be traced to within the lifetimes of those who knew him.

Fact three: The people who spread these ideas, far from seeming loony, began to live in a new way—a way that transformed human history.

Whatever else we might say about Jesus, at least these facts are beyond serious debate. We can show, even to the standards of modern historians, that these three things happened. How does a modern person, especially one who does not want to accept miracles and rising from the dead as real possibilities, make sense of these facts?

Why did it happen? Why did this one man of the Roman world, and no other, become identified by so many as God—not *a* god, mind you, but *the* God? Why did people come so quickly to view his every word and action as sacred? Why did they go out, everywhere, to share his startling new teachings about forgiveness, love, peace, and bodily resurrection?

Modern people have found many ways to respond to this strange set of facts, but the responses can be arranged, for the most part, into three categories. Taken together, these categories broadly cover the ways people today deal with Jesus. After we have examined them, we will have a better vantage point from which to examine the biographical details and the themes of his life.

The Standard Modern View of Jesus

The standard modern view of Jesus, what we could call the secular view, involves a collection of guesses that modern people make as to how the stories about Jesus as a divine miracle-worker who rose from the dead developed.

Modern secular guesses at "what really happened" include:

1. *Mass Delusion*—Jesus was a charismatic preacher (perhaps of the kind we sometimes see in cult leaders) who aroused apocalyptic hopes in his followers. When he was killed, they suffered a mass delusion, a group hysteria, or some similar thing that made them cling to the idea that he had risen from the dead. From this hysteria, or delusion, all the wild stories about Jesus were born.

2. *Lying*—Early Christian leaders and writers made up stories, or fantastically embellished ordinary things Jesus did, to trick people.

3. *Mythologizing*—Jesus lived and died as a normal rabbi, or maybe just as a ragged preacher, but over time, the stories about him got bigger and bigger until they were basically myths. From the kernel of a real man's life grew this great mythology now known as Christianity.

4. *Non-literalness*—The stories told about Jesus in the decades after his death are actually spiritual lessons meant to share his message of love. They are not literal accounts of things that actually happened. Jesus did not literally rise from the dead, for example; rather, such talk is a stylized manner of speaking meant to convey the life-giving spiritual power of his teaching.

Unfortunately, none of these guesses, by itself, is particularly convincing.

The beliefs of these new Christians, such as the teaching

that God is love, or the moral commands to care for the poor and sick, or the social teaching of the equality of everyone before God, do not seem to be the work of delusional people or liars. We consider them sane, admirable.

There doesn't seem to have been enough time between the death of Jesus and the writing of the first Gospel, around thirty years later, for grandiose myths to have developed organically. And there would have been too many people alive who still remembered him and could have corrected those who made up stories about him.

And the idea of the Jesus stories being merely a set of spiritual lessons, not meant to be taken literally, doesn't seem to fit with the evidence that so many people—including his closest followers—died defending the stories as literally true.

Still, even though no single one of these guesses is really satisfactory, for some people they do serve as adequate placeholder explanations. *After all*, they might say, *the story of Jesus is a very strange event that happened a long time ago. We can't know what actually happened, so what probably happened was something like this . . .* (insert your guesses here). Perhaps they convince themselves that two or three inadequate guesses add up to one good one.

This strategy of vaguely assembling various guesses might make sense to some people, given that most don't have the time or energy to investigate every religious claim. But in this book, we are taking the time, at least once, to fully investigate the claim, and so we have to admit that these guesses really are just guesses, and they're not great.

We must also admit that the reason, at least in many cases, for relying on these guesses is that many modern people have decided that things like God and miracles do not exist. That is to say, the motive for making these guesses in the first place is that so many modern people have given up on God, miracles, heaven, angels, and every other divine thing.

And if we have given up on God, then we assume that Jesus cannot be God, which means the three solid facts we have about him—that he lived, that those who knew him claimed he was divine, and that these people gave the world a beautiful and transformative new way of life—are just an unexplainable quirk of history.

The New Age View of Jesus

While many modern people have become mentally hardened against religious claims, other modern people have reacted to increased secularization of the world in the opposite way. They have become enthusiastic explorers of the spiritual life, trying to cultivate spiritual experiences that will make the world less cold and routine. In Eastern mysticism, in paganism, and even in the occult, people seek to explore and restore the side of life that has been overwhelmed by the mechanical, the technological, the processed, and the manufactured.

Such people tend to be open to a great variety of spiritual claims, often seeking to locate general spiritual laws (such as, in our day, the "Law of Attraction" or the "Law of

Reciprocity") that they believe operate within all the religions and spiritualities of the world. For them, the world is a religious buffet from which they assemble an appetizing plate of spiritual delicacies. The appeal of this eclectic cafeteria-style approach to religion, from which we can take whatever we find helpful, is easy to see. After all, if we're trying to grasp divine things, why not try to glean what we can from all the ages of human spiritual thought and practice?

But this approach has a crushing dark side: it turns many people into spiritual predators who, rather than respecting all religions, put themselves above all religions as the judges of what is worth keeping and what must be discarded. It also promotes dilettantism, trapping people in a life of constant searching after new spiritual experiences and tidbits of interesting knowledge rather than devoting themselves to the hard work of real searching for (and abiding by) truth.

Such people may also refuse to close off possibilities, making them impervious to the truth. Instead of saying "no" to falsity, as truth requires, they pretend that all things are true if you just see them from a higher level. They spin around and around in ambiguity, and they tell themselves that their refusal to finally say "no" to false religion and "yes" to true religion makes them, somehow, enlightened and open-minded rather than ridiculous.

This generalized spirituality, a common component of what is often called the New Age Movement, mostly deals with Jesus by categorizing him as one of history's wise and enlightened teachers. He is yet another dish in the great buffet of wisdom, not fundamentally different from all the other delights to be tasted.

The spiritual entrepreneur Deepak Chopra gives us an example of this treatment of Jesus in the author's note to his novel *Jesus: A Story of Enlightenment*. "How Jesus came to be united with God was a process that happened in the mind," Chopra writes. "Seen from the perspective of Buddha or the ancient rishis ('seers') of India, Jesus attained enlightenment."

A first thing that now must strike us about such an approach is that it is almost exactly the opposite of what Jesus claimed about himself.

A second thing is that such an interpretation requires us to believe that Jesus' own followers did not understand him as well as the modern spiritual guide (like himself) now does. The guide, as Chopra does, makes *himself* the explainer of what Jesus "really" meant when he identified himself with God.

The fact that many teachings of Jesus are logically incompatible with the teachings of other religions on the buffet, such as Hinduism and Buddhism, is explained away or ignored, making the attempt to harmonize Jesus' teaching with someone's favored "spiritual laws" always seem to result in an image of Jesus that is remarkably like a modern New Age teacher! This co-opts Jesus into a kind of spokesman for modern teachings, which hardly seems to respect his place as a world-transforming figure who was perfectly capable of speaking for himself.

The Traditional Christian View

This view is comparatively simple: the things written in the Gospels—Matthew, Mark, Luke, and John—are memories of things that really happened, and they have been organized and worded by each Gospel writer to convey accurately who Jesus was and what he did.

Centuries of scholarship have gone into trying to fully understand the processes and personalities behind the creation of these works and to pinpoint the dates and circumstances of authorship. But leaving aside such specifics, in the traditional Christian view, each Gospel is an attempt to put in writing the key details of Jesus' life for the community, the *ecclesia* in Greek, that Jesus had established and that his apostles and disciples were, at that time, building up everywhere.

That is the context of the Gospels. Immediately after the death of Jesus, the institution that he founded, his *ecclesia*, became very active in taking his story, his teaching, and his practices to as many people as possible. His *ecclesia* had a clear structure, with apostles as leaders and with Peter as first among the apostles. The members of this *ecclesia* also had a set of practices such as baptism, a sacred memorial meal, anointing of the sick with oils, and various other things that Jesus had tasked them with carrying on. And this *ecclesia* believed that Jesus was God.

This well-organized and steadily growing community provided the context for the writing of the Gospels. This organization, headed by the apostles and, soon after, by those appointed by the apostles, approved of and accepted these four Gospels. It used them in its teaching about Jesus, especially when it gathered each Sunday for the memorial.

During the time of the writing of the earliest books of the New Testament, this community had within it hundreds, probably thousands, of people who had seen and heard Jesus. It had leaders who had spent years following Jesus and being instructed by him. And this communal reality gives each of the Gospels an *authenticity.* The Gospel writers meant to get the story right because their community was based on that story, and the many eyewitnesses or students of witnesses among them were able to help them get it right.

Here's how Luke, for example, says he came to write his biography of Jesus:

Inasmuch as many have undertaken to compile a narrative of the things which have been accomplished among us, just as they were delivered to us by those who from the beginning were eyewitnesses and ministers of the word, it seemed good to me also, having followed all things closely for some time past, to write an orderly account for you . . . that you may know the truth concerning the things of which you have been informed (Luke 1:1–4).

Christians today believe that all the Gospel authors set out to tell the unembellished truth as the Church that Jesus founded remembered it, and therefore that they're reliable.

This is my view, and it will influence everything that follows in this book. I do not dismiss the ancient people as unreliable simply because they were ancient and make up my own guesses about "what really happened." Nor do I treat Jesus as just another spiritual teacher, a thing he clearly denied about himself. Rather, I take the early Christian writings to be the memories of eyewitnesses written down either by those eyewitnesses or by people who knew them. I take these eyewitnesses and writers to be serious people, gravely devoted to a radical new teaching of truth, forgiveness, peace, and love. I accept the evidence that this new teaching brought beauty and goodness into the lives of those who followed it, into the entire Roman world, and across twenty centuries into the world today.

Further, I believe that all of this is a work of God, whose power ensured that the Gospels were filled with truth and kept free of distortion.

With confidence in the good intentions and the inspired witness of the early Christian writers, we can take the Gospels seriously—and now begin our look at the details of Jesus' life that are contained within them.

Jesus: Emmanuel and Savior

The name *Jesus* is also a title. It is an English transliteration of a Hebrew word made up of two parts, one of which is the Jewish name for "God" and the other of which is the Hebrew word for "saves." Thus, Jesus means "God Saves."

Jesus gets his name directly from an angel who tells Joseph that Mary is pregnant and instructs Joseph, "You shall call his name Jesus, for he will save his people from their sins" (Matt. 1:21). But in the very next line of his Gospel, Matthew tells us, "All this took place to fulfil what the Lord had spoken by the prophet: 'Behold, a virgin shall conceive and bear a son, and his name shall be called Emmanuel' (which means, God with us)" (Matt. 1:22–23).

So, Matthew is saying that the prophecy of Isaiah—that the Messiah will be called *Emmanuel*—is actually fulfilled when the angel tells Joseph to name the child Jesus. This is not a contradiction. The idea in Isaiah is not so much that the literal name of the Messiah will be Emmanuel, but that "God is with us" will be applicable to him. And the name *Jesus* conveys the same idea, but with the added dimension of salvation. The God who is with us, Jesus, is with us to save us from sin and death, which is more than even Isaiah likely hoped for.

His personal name is Jesus. That will be his name forever. But the meaning of his life to those who come to know him is Emmanuel: "God is with us." He is God who has come to be with us and save us.

5

An Expected Life

Jesus was expected. By the time of his birth, in fact, people had been expecting him for hundreds of years. This is one of the many factors marking Jesus as special in all of history. What other person can claim to have been born to a people who had been awaiting him for centuries?

We see evidence of this expectation in many of the questions that people asked Jesus. John the Baptist, for example, wanted to know, "Are you the one who is to come, or should we expect someone else?" (Matt. 11:3).

John's question refers to the *Messiah*, or "anointed one," a mysterious figure (or, for some, possibly *figures*) popularly expected by the Jews of Jesus' time, based on prophecies in the Jewish scriptures. For example, early in Jewish history, God told Moses to tell the people, "I will raise up for them a prophet like you from among their brethren; and I will put my words in his mouth, and he shall speak to them all that I command him (Deut. 18:18).

And then centuries after Moses, sometime around the year 1000 B.C., God gave them David as their greatest king.

God promised to David, "Your house and your kingdom shall be made sure for ever before me; your throne shall be established for ever" (2 Sam. 7:16).

From these two promises, supported by many other passages in Scripture, the Jews came to expect that a great prophet would be sent to them as well as a final and eternal king who would be a descendant of David.

The prophecies in the book of Isaiah (composed in the 500s B.C. at the latest, and probably much earlier) described the one whom God would send. Many of these prophecies became familiar to every Jewish person, and, indeed, they have become some of the best-known texts in history—giving us such common phrases as "they shall beat their swords into ploughshares" and familiar prophecies such as:

> The wolf shall dwell with the lamb,
> and the leopard shall lie down with the kid,
> and the calf and the lion and the fatling together,
> and a little child shall lead them (Isa. 11:6).

In many cases, in our day Isaiah's prophecies might easily be mistaken for New Testament references to Jesus, such as:

> For to us a child is born,
> to us a son is given;
> and the government will be upon his shoulder,
> and his name will be called

"Wonderful Counselor, Mighty God,
Everlasting Father, Prince of Peace" (Isa. 9:6).

Throughout the Jewish scriptures we find many other references to the one who is to come. There is no reasonable way to understand Jewish history, in fact, without accounting for all the messianic predictions and prophecies that the Jews reported to have received.

Now of course, prophecy lends itself to various interpretations, and skeptical scholars today argue about just how much the Old Testament prophecies can be taken to refer to Jesus, or to any Messiah at all. But we don't need to delve into modern scholarly skepticism here because what cannot be denied is that the Jewish people in the time of Jesus were alert with expectation for the Messiah.

And Jesus, in many of the things he did, met the expectations. This raised such intense emotions that sometimes Jesus had to tamp down the excitement. According to John's Gospel, after Jesus performed a miracle to feed a crowd of 5,000, the people said, "'This is indeed the prophet who is to come into the world!' Perceiving then that they were about to come and take him by force to make him king, Jesus withdrew again to the hills by himself" (John 6:14–15).

We should mention one other thing here about Jewish expectations for the Messiah. Even if no prophecy of the Messiah had ever been made, by its very nature and structure Judaism would still be a religion of waiting for and expecting a moment of triumph for God. For Jews, evil was not part of the world God made. Evil entered the world later because people chose to turn away from God. The Jewish religion is based in the idea that God—who made everything good—has a plan for rescuing humanity from the harm done by its choice to turn from him and restoring everything to goodness.

In Jesus' time, every believing Jew awaited the day when this plan would be complete and all things would be set right. What is more, they understood themselves to be central to God's plan. God had promised Abraham, the father of the Jewish people, that "by your descendants shall all the nations of the earth bless themselves, because you have obeyed my voice" (Gen. 22:18). This meant that the Jewish relationship with God had as its purpose the restoration of "all the nations" to the "blessed" state of correct and healthy relationship with God.

God, in time, was going to make this happen. He was going to bless all the nations, and he was going to accomplish it through the Jewish people.

Throughout history, God made a series of *covenants* with the Jewish people, holy pacts that drew them closer to himself, making them better and better able to live up to the call of being a blessing to the nations. And through the prophet Jeremiah, he promised them that, one day, he would institute a new covenant:

> But this is the covenant which I will make with the house of Israel after those days, says the LORD: I will put my law within them, and I will write it upon their hearts; and I will be their God, and they shall be my people. And

no longer shall each man teach his neighbor and each his brother, saying, "Know the LORD," for they shall all know me, from the least of them to the greatest, says the LORD; for I will forgive their iniquity, and I will remember their sin no more (Jer. 31:33–34).

Their centuries of relationship with God filled the Jewish people with confidence that, having been called and set apart by him, so long as they remained faithful to him they would play a central part in his plan to restore the world, and they would be rewarded for their efforts.

God would have his final triumph, and they, as his chosen people, would triumph with him.

This is an entirely different view of history from the polytheistic views that flourished in all the other cultures around the Jews. In their religions, there was no plan to bless all the nations and to transform human hearts. Among the pagans of the ancient world, their many gods simply struggled for power and one never knew for sure how those struggles would turn out. The best a person could do was offer sacrifices in the hopes that the gods would do good things instead of evil.

For the Jews, though, God promised that justice and mercy would one day triumph. This Jewish way of thinking about history represented a leap forward for humanity.

In fact, if there is one clear difference between the ancient world and the modern world, it is that the Jewish view of history *won*. To the degree that we modern people believe that history has a trajectory, that it makes progress toward greater justice and mercy, we are deeply driven by the Jewish—not the pagan—view of history.

The prophecies of the Messiah are part of this larger expectation. For the everyday Jewish person in the time of Jesus, the Messiah would usher in the age of the new covenant promised to Jeremiah. That takes on great significance when Jesus, at the end of his life, refers to his own blood as "my blood of the covenant, which is poured out for many for the forgiveness of sins" (Matt. 26:28).

Sent by God, the Messiah would be a prophet greater than Moses and a king greater than David, and through him, the world would enter into a new and permanent covenant with God and be restored to correct relationship with him.

All of this is what John the Baptist is referring to when he asks his fateful question, "Are you he who is to come, or shall we look for another?" (Luke 7:19).

In response, Jesus says, "The blind receive their sight, the lame walk, lepers are cleansed, and the deaf hear, the dead are raised up, the poor have good news preached to them" (Luke 7:22).

To us, it may seem like a strange way to answer the question. But here, Jesus is invoking well-known messianic prophecies. For example, one from Isaiah says,

Say to those who are of a fearful heart,
"Be strong, fear not!
Behold, your God
will come with vengeance,

with the recompense of God.
He will come and save you."
Then the eyes of the blind shall be opened,
and the ears of the deaf unstopped;
then shall the lame man leap like a hart,
and the tongue of the dumb sing for joy" (Isa. 35:4–6).

Another comes from Psalm 146:

The LORD sets the prisoners free;
the LORD opens the eyes of the blind.
The LORD lifts up those who are bowed down;
the LORD loves the righteous.
The LORD watches over the sojourners,
he upholds the widow and the fatherless;
but the way of the wicked he brings to ruin (Psalm 146: 7–9).

Jesus is unique among all those ever born into this world. His coming was described in detail hundreds of years before he was born, and he was longed for by generations. As he went about teaching and healing and casting out demons, he showed himself to be the Messiah whom the Jews awaited. And with his coming, the long-promised age of restoration dawned in town after town. As Jesus put it to those who questioned where his power comes from: "The kingdom of God has come upon you" (Luke 11:20).

Jesus: Christ and Lord

Christ, from the Greek word *christos*, and Messiah, from the Hebrew word *masia,* both mean "anointed." In the ancient world, anointing with oil could have a variety of meanings—from invoking healing on the sick to confirming someone as a king. For this reason, many people could be called messiahs or christs.

But the use of the word *Christ* after the name of Jesus invokes, quite specifically, the tradition of the Davidic Messiah, the descendant of David whose reign would restore all things. To call him Christ is a statement of faith in him as the Davidic Messiah, the most important and holy person in history.

Perhaps surprisingly, this does not necessarily include the claim that Jesus is God. (All throughout history there have been people who accepted the claim that Jesus is the Jewish Messiah but rejected the claim that he is God.) To make clear that he was not just Messiah, but also God, his early followers used the title *Lord*.

Like *Messiah*, the word *Lord* can be applied to different people in different situations. But in the case of the earliest followers of Jesus, who were almost all Jews, to call Jesus "Lord" is not to use the word in a general sense, but in the sense of the Jewish tradition of calling *God* "Lord."

Because the name of God is holy to Jews—so holy as to be inutterable—when writing and speaking they commonly replace it with other words, usually with *Lord* (in Hebrew,

Adonai). This tradition informs the use of this word by his early Jewish followers.

There are christs and lords of many kinds, but when these words are applied to Jesus, they invoke very specific traditions and a specific meaning. To call Jesus "Messiah and Lord," is to make very specific claims about him—that he is the expected descendant of David, and that he—as shocking as this reality may be—is God.

6

Our First Moment with Jesus: The Shepherds, the Angels, and the Good News

Jesus was the long-awaited Messiah who came to usher in the kingdom of God. But what was he like as a person? How did he live, and what did he do?

For answers to these questions we turn, primarily, to the Gospels. For some people, reading the Gospels can seem like a chore. I find this to be the case for two main reasons:

1. The world of the Gospels is long gone, so it can take some work to learn the people, places, and circumstances in which the stories of Jesus unfold.

2. The beliefs of the Jews are central to the story of Jesus, so without some familiarity with the Old Testament we can

miss a lot of the significance of what Jesus does and what happens to him.

One relatively easy way to minimize these problems is to read from a New Testament that includes helpful commentary. Another is to read in a group with other people who can help fill in the details about Judaism and the ancient world.

We're going to keep things very simple here by focusing on a few personal interactions with Jesus, so that we can get to know him before moving on to what he did and, finally, to why people still follow him. Fortunately, the structure of the Gospels makes this easy. Although each of the four Gospels can be read as a long story, a book with a beginning, a middle, and an end, they are also structured to be read as collections of little encounters with Jesus.

In fact, this is how Christians have always read the Gospels, meditating on them one bit at a time. Today, just as in the earliest days of Christianity, the community listens together, especially at the Sunday gathering, to one of these Gospel moments. (They are meant to be shared by a community as part of the communal worship of God.) Then, together, the community meditates on this moment through preaching and inward listening.

Each of the Gospel vignettes about Jesus is a real event. We should not think of them merely as pious stories. But we, the readers of the Gospels, are meant to enter each moment meditatively as an opportunity to experience the mystery of God in Jesus.

I have chosen six moments for us to meditate on in the next few chapters. Let us begin at the beginning, the moment of his birth. In Luke's Gospel, immediately after Jesus is born, Mary places him in the manger, and then this happens:

> And in that region there were shepherds out in the field, keeping watch over their flock by night. And an angel of the Lord appeared to them, and the glory of the Lord shone around them, and they were filled with fear. And the angel said to them, "Be not afraid; for behold, I bring you good news of a great joy which will come to all the people; for to you is born this day in the city of David a Savior, who is Christ the Lord. And this will be a sign for you: you will find a babe wrapped in swaddling cloths and lying in a manger." And suddenly there was with the angel a multitude of the heavenly host praising God and saying, "Glory to God in the highest, and on earth peace among men with whom he is pleased!" (Luke 2:8–14).

This moment is full of foreshadowing about Jesus' life. Luke, the careful historian, gives it to us as an opportunity, right at the beginning of his biography, to reflect deeply on who Jesus is. The fact that Jesus is announced by an angel shows his divine importance, for example. The fact that the announcement is given to lowly shepherds shows that this Messiah and Lord has come to be a gift to ordinary people. And the contrast between the darkness into which Jesus is born and the glory of God that shines around the shepherds is an image of the meaning of his life. Jesus is light in the darkness.

What is more, that the world is *asleep* at the moment of his birth is an image of its spiritual sleep, its deadness to spiritual things. Only the poor shepherds are awake, and their lonely midnight vigil gives the story an instructive eeriness. Suddenly, the shining truth about the world is unveiled before them. Angels are in their midst, and it is both wonderful and terrifying.

This, Luke is telling us, is the reality of the human situation, though we are mostly numb to it. The world of divine things is right here, in our midst, and we would be as overwhelmed as the shepherds if it suddenly opened up around us.

So much is happening on so many levels in these few lines of Luke's Gospel that we could meditate on them for many pages. But for the moment I would like to focus only on a few words of the angel and what they tell us about Jesus: "I bring you good news of great joy."

Any serious attempt to understand who Jesus was and what he was like must explore the ancient Christian idea of "good news." This phrase, which appears as far back as the prophecies of Isaiah in the Old Testament and which is proclaimed here by an angel at the moment of Jesus' birth, is always at the heart of what Jesus does.

In fact, the English word *gospel* is a translation of the Greek *euangelion*, which means "good news."

As we have seen, Jesus began his own public ministry by proclaiming, "The time is fulfilled, and the kingdom of God is at hand; repent, and believe in the gospel [good news]" (Mark 1:15). After his death and resurrection, the Church he founded then took up the task of proclaiming good news.

With these words we have a key for understanding him.

The modern world often regards the Christian message as bad news. It is bad news because it comes with lots of life-style demands. It is bad news because it seems out of date. And it is bad news because some people have been hurt by Christian institutions or in the name of Christ.

The story of how the original spirit of excitement at the good news of Jesus came to be treated as bad news has many twists and turns. For now, it is enough to remember that there was a time when Jesus generated a massive outpouring of emotion and fervor as he went from town to town proclaiming good news. And after Jesus had gone, the apostles and disciples understood themselves to be carrying on the mission of Jesus by bringing his good news to the whole world.

So what is the "good news," and what does it tell us about who Jesus was?

One way of understanding the meaning of good news is simply that Jesus was the Messiah, the promised one of God. This certainly qualifies as good news. But there are deeper levels of meaning to explore as well.

Consider what Jesus says in the Gospel of Mark: "The time is fulfilled, and the kingdom of God is at hand; repent, and believe in the gospel [*euangelion*]" (Mark 1:15). Jesus is declaring that something has happened, and he is telling you what you should do about it.

What has happened? "The time is fulfilled, and the kingdom of God is at hand."

What should you do about it? "Repent and believe in the gospel."

This proclamation claims that the entire history of the Jews, and, in fact, the entire history of humanity, has been, up to this point, the time of waiting. But now that is over. Now has come the time for all things to be set right and for God to rule.

There is a candid realism about the word *repent* in this context. We humans adjust to our time and place, and the people to whom Jesus speaks have, undoubtedly, made many moral accommodations in order to succeed in a harsh and sinful world. What is more, they have not yet been fully instructed in how a human life is really meant to be lived. For them, the full instructions would only come with the Messiah. As one woman tells Jesus, before she knows who he is, "I know that Messiah is coming (he who is called Christ); when he comes, he will show us all things" (John 4:25). Thus, even the best people must repent when they meet Jesus. In the absence of full instruction they have done what they could, but now the instructor is here, and they must give up the old ways for the new.

Saying "repent," is the equivalent of saying, "Now that something new is happening, shake yourself awake, give up your old ways of dealing with the world, and turn, now, to the new thing. Believe in it—that is how you can be part of it." Repenting is a two-part action, like stepping through a doorway. With the same step, we both leave the old room and enter the new.

Leaving the old room is essential. It must be done. The person hearing the message of Jesus must come to rely on what Jesus says and trust what he is saying.

The Gospels tell of Jesus announcing this message in many places, sometimes with slight variations in the wording. And these variations are important. Sometimes the "good news" is that the *time* of the kingdom of God has arrived. Sometimes the "good news" is that the kingdom of God is moving through *space*. For example, Luke reports Jesus as instructing his apostles to "heal the sick . . . and say to them, 'The kingdom of God has come near to you'" (Luke 10:8–9).

With Jesus, the kingdom of God is both *dawning in time* and *moving in space*.

At this point, we can say something about the deeper meanings of the term *good news*. With Jesus, the kingdom of God has *physically* come. It is physically present because Jesus, himself, represents the presence of the kingdom of God.

This is something that is often misinterpreted by those who want to syncretize the teachings of Jesus with the teachings of other "spiritual masters." There is a tendency to think that what Jesus is teaching is merely something like, "Everyone has the kingdom of God within." And at a certain level, this does fit with Jesus' teaching about the importance of the inner life.

But that is not what Jesus means. "The kingdom of God has come upon you" is not merely a spiritual statement; it is also, and most importantly, a statement about who he is—God. In him, God has entered space and time.

This is the fullness of the meaning of the good news. And, if we go back and look at the original proclamation of the angel to the shepherds, now we can see it clearly: "for to you is born this day in the city of David a Savior, who is Christ the Lord."

Not just Christ, but "Christ the Lord."

God, himself, has come.

Years later, the apostle Paul would refer to Jesus as "the image of the invisible God" (Col. 1:15). If we try to imagine what it was like for those who saw him and heard him speak, we must not let go of these words. When we see Jesus, we see what God is like.

What is shocking about God, as we see him in Jesus, is not the power as shown in the miracles. Of course God has power. Of course God can do miracles. Rather, what is truly shocking is that God is humble. This is the deepest and strangest part of the good news. God has come, and he is not what people expected. He is the opposite of the rulers of this world.

Jesus gives us the most precise and touching description of himself when he implores his followers, "Come to me, all who labor and are heavy laden, and I will give you rest. Take my yoke upon you, and learn from me; for I am gentle and lowly in heart, and you will find rest for your souls. For my yoke is easy, and my burden is light" (Matt. 11:28–30).

This understanding of God as humble was foundational in early Christianity. In the teaching of this surprising, humble God, they were given the key to how they were to live. Here is the apostle Paul instructing Christians in how to live by sharing with them a hymn to the humility of God:

Have this mind among yourselves, which was in Christ Jesus, who, though he was in the form of God, did not count equality with God a thing to be grasped, but emptied himself, taking the form of a servant, being born in the likeness of men. And being found in human form he humbled himself and became obedient unto death, even death on a cross. Therefore God has highly exalted him and bestowed on him the name which is above every name, that at the name of Jesus every knee should bow, in heaven and on earth and under the earth, and every tongue confess that Jesus Christ is Lord, to the glory of God the Father" (Phil. 2:5–11).

The glory of God is found in his willingness to be the servant of others. God's will is to be the servant of my happiness, if only I will let him love me.

Because of his humility, those who were ill-treated by society knew themselves to be safe with him. Those who felt cut off from God understood themselves to be welcomed by him. No one—not even outcasts such as lepers—was outside of his concern or unwelcome as his friend.

It is impossible to overstate the power of Jesus' humility. It is, mysteriously, his greatest power. It is in his humility that he accomplishes the one task he seems to most want to accomplish—to share God's life with everyone. By making himself low, he makes himself accessible to all.

If we want to understand his personality, so to speak, this is the quality that most marks him: his humble willingness—his unquenchable desire—to share his life with others. He goes to parties and dinners as freely as he goes out to the desolate places. He is sociable and kind. He loves to tell stories. He eats and drinks without fussing. And though he is a deeply moral person himself, he does not hold himself apart from those who live loosely.

Jesus never denies his superior nature; he insists on it. His bluntness about this fact can be grating when we first encounter it in the Gospels. When he tells people things like, "You are from below; I am from above. You are of this world; I am not of this world" (John 8:23), we want to respond, "Who does this guy think he is?"

But these statements are not arrogant. They, too, are acts of humility on his part because he knows that saying such things annoys many people and opens him up to hatred and derision. But he says them because people have to know who he is. If they do not know, he cannot give them what he came to give them, which is a share in the divine life. Everywhere he goes, he makes clear that he wants to share his life with others, just as friends share life together. But the life he shares is truly life, eternal life, because he is God. Letting people know who he is makes it possible for them to accept what he is offering: friendship and shared life with God.

This is the good news. In Jesus, God has come, and he is humble. What a great relief this news is to a world that has not known God or thought it possible to be his friend.

God Prepares the Jews

In John's Gospel, Jesus says that "salvation is from the Jews" (John 4:22).

With this little phrase, he affirms that the Jews are not like any other people, nation, or religion. They have been set apart by God for the purpose of saving the world (a reality that often led to their being resented, and even hated, by the world).

Their story began in roughly 1600 B.C., when the man we know as Abraham was called out of his homeland (probably in modern day Iraq or Turkey) to found a new nation. For a time, Abraham's descendants remained a shepherd people of little note. Down through the centuries, however, under the leadership of prophets and kings, they became a people of immeasurable influence. From them, the world received an entirely new kind of religion.

They are renowned for their monotheism, the belief in one supreme God, but this word can hardly do justice to the new religion that God gave the world through them. It was an entirely new way of relating to the divine. They understood nature as no people ever had before. They understood time as no people had before. They understood the moral law as no people had before. And all of this was because they understood themselves to have been called out from among the nations by the creator of the universe.

To them, the natural world was an intentional creation of a creator God who filled it with goodness. To them, history was the story of humanity's separation from the goodness of God and God's promises and his actions to restore all things. And to them, God was not remote, but an active and demanding defender of the righteous and opponent of injustice.

Through the various covenants that God made with them, and through the teachings of their prophets across the centuries, they came to have a unique understanding of the goodness of the Creator and of his creation. They also came to understand that the Creator had a plan for history, one that would see justice and goodness triumph in the end. And, finally, they came to have an understanding of a moral law that prioritized God and neighbor over all other values.

They had the commandments not to kill, or steal, or commit adultery that might have made sense to persons of other ancient religions. But they also had the commandment to honor only the one God, which no other people had. And, perhaps most strangely, they had the final two of the ten commandments: the commandments not to "covet" people or objects.

These commandments further demonstrate the uniqueness of the Jews as a people. For they had a God who cared about not just what they did but *who they were on the inside*. Their God was profoundly interested in meeting them not just in the temple, but in their interior lives. Through the prophet Ezekiel, their God had said, "A new heart I will give you, and a new spirit I will put within you; and I will take out of your flesh the heart of stone and give you a heart of flesh" (Ezek. 36:26).

Their acceptance of God within their hearts and minds prepared the way for Jesus, who taught a religion of radical interior transformation when he said such things as, "But I say to you that every one who is angry with his brother shall be liable to judgment" (Matt. 5:22).

Had Jesus come to any other people, his life, his suffering, and his death would not have been understood. Most especially, his death would not have been understood as a sacrifice to take away sin and to restore humanity to right relationship with God. Outside of the Jewish context, Jesus' most central teachings would falter, including his teachings about self-giving love.

Jews had a religion of love for more than a thousand years before Jesus came, having been told by Moses, "You shall not hate your brother in your heart, but you shall reason with your neighbor, lest you bear sin because of him. You shall not take vengeance or bear any grudge against the sons of your own people, but you shall love your neighbor as yourself" (Lev. 19:17–18).

Through his loving and fatherly relationship with the Jews, God changed the spiritual landscape of the world. The Jewish people are his special possession, and their teaching about the nature of God made it possible for the world to accept Jesus when he came.

7

Our Second Moment with Jesus: A Boy in the Temple of God

The temple in Jerusalem was one of the most impressive buildings of the ancient world. And, although it functioned as a place of ritual sacrifice and prayer, it was also a place of study, the center of a vast network of Jewish schools and synagogues that stretched throughout the Roman world and beyond. This network of institutions around the empire presented a compelling alternative to paganism, and through it many Gentiles came to accept the one God.

Whether you were a Jew or a gentile, if you wanted to devote yourself to learning about the God of Israel from the greatest minds and the most respectable schools of thought, you went to the temple in Jerusalem. During the life of Jesus, the great teachers Hillel and Shammai taught the Jewish law at the temple. In fact, they might have been there when, just on the cusp of adulthood, Jesus found his way to the temple:

Now his parents went to Jerusalem every year at the feast of the Passover. And when he was twelve years old, they went up according to custom; and when the feast was ended, as they were returning, the boy Jesus stayed behind in Jerusalem. His parents did not know it, but supposing him to be in the company they went a day's journey, and they sought him among their kinsfolk and acquaintances; and when they did not find him, they returned to Jerusalem, seeking him.

After three days they found him in the temple, sitting among the teachers, listening to them and asking them questions; and all who heard him were amazed at his understanding and his answers. And when they saw him they were astonished; and his mother said to him, "Son, why have you treated us so? Behold, your father and I have been looking for you anxiously." And he said to them, "How is it that you sought me? Did you not know that I must be in my Father's house?"

And they did not understand the saying which he spoke to them. And he went down with them and came to Nazareth, and was obedient to them; and his mother kept all these things in her heart. And Jesus increased in wisdom and in stature, and in favor with God and man (Luke 2:41–52).

Because travel in the ancient world was not always safe, the trip to Jerusalem from Galilee would have been made with a caravan of people, something like a wagon train crossing the Old West. Jesus missed the caravan as it headed home, probably because he had something more he needed to accomplish in Jerusalem. He knew that once his parents noticed that he was not with the group, they would come back looking for him.

And where should they look? Considering what they knew about him from the events of his early life, including the announcements of angels, they should have known that the temple was the logical place for him to go.

As he waited, he entered the religious debates of the wise men at the temple, the world's leaders in Jewish thought. We are not told what he said, and there seems to be a good reason for this. Luke seems to have gotten the story from Mary, the mother of Jesus, because it is told from her perspective. She and Joseph walked in and saw him "sitting among the teachers, listening to them and asking them questions."

Perhaps they rushed up to Jesus, and, as they collected him to go home, the scholars said something like, "That's quite a son you have; he has been astounding us with his understanding and his answers."

Even though there's no report of what Jesus actually said, this story is valuable because it fills in biographical facts we would not otherwise know. This is the last story that involves his father Joseph, for example, and it is our only indication that Joseph was alive to raise him beyond infancy.

We also see that his family was religiously observant, and that, although they may have been poor by our standards, they were not destitute. They had the money to go to Jerusalem every year, after all.

We see that he spoke frankly and in a mature way with his parents, but also in a way that makes him slightly strange to them. Even in a society in which a twelve-year-old is trusted with a great deal of responsibility, and is much closer to the full responsibility of adulthood than a child of twelve would be today, his reply to his parents is surprisingly manly: "How is it that you sought me? Did you not know that I must be in my Father's house?"

This is not a child asking the forgiveness of his parents or even reassuring them after their fright. This is a young man who knows who he is and who expects his parents to know as well.

In our modern context we might read this as a kid being too big for his britches and maybe even mouthing off a bit. But in his context, that does not explain his response. A more likely reading is that he truly required more understanding from them. After all that had happened (angels, dreams, wise men, shepherds, etc.) it was long past time for them to fully understand that he was filled with power and that nothing would happen to him that was not the will of heaven.

The question, "Did you not know?" carries with it the implication that they did know, but that they had not yet allowed the knowledge to fully settle in their minds. They were still reserving judgment, at least in some part of themselves, about what all of this meant. Some part of them still focused on him as their little boy more clearly than it focused on him as the Son of God.

The Son of God had been entrusted to them, and now, he needed them to surrender that heavy burden. Without doubt, part of the reason for his staying in Jerusalem was that he intended to move his own parents beyond their fears for his safety. He arranged the situation so that they could begin to let him go.

In fact, as a twelve-year-old male, he almost certainly had the right to stay in Jerusalem if he wanted. But by asserting his right in the way he did, he allowed things to develop for his parents' benefit. He allowed a drama to unfold that, even if they did not understand it at the time, changed all of their roles. He moved from the role of protected child into the role of teacher and savior. They moved from the role of protectors into the role of followers who must trust his choices. Once this change in roles was accomplished, he was able to return home with them and obey them, confident that they would no longer confuse his obedience with vulnerability.

Otherwise, if they had continued to think of him as a vulnerable child, his obedience would have become a source of hurt to them. It would have left them feeling that they were stuck with an impossible job: keeping God safe.

It was time for that burden to be taken off their shoulders.

Joseph's role, in particular—because it was the role of a physical protector—now shifted from the one who must be trustworthy to the one who must simply trust. By staying behind in Jerusalem, Jesus was preparing for Joseph's death. Had Jesus not demonstrated to his parents that he was ready to take up responsibility for his own life, would Joseph have been able to die in peace, leaving Jesus and Mary behind?

The story of the boy Jesus in the temple also allows us insights we would not otherwise have into Jesus' personality and development.

His spiritual genius is already manifest, even at twelve. He is already well versed in Scripture or he would not have been able to engage in the kinds of discussions that were central to the temple schools. His awareness that he is the Messiah is already present because he calls the temple "my Father's house." And his role as a teacher, or *rabbi*, is already present because he asks questions. Rabbis of this time used questioning of students and other scholars as their primary method of teaching.

From all of this, an image emerges of the young Jesus as an engaging and brilliant child, with loving parents and a normal life. He was confident in his interactions with his elders, but he was obedient to his parents, and, though he was clearly unusual in his intellectual abilities, he learned and grew just like any other person.

It would be centuries before Christians would develop the language to explain how Jesus could be God but also be a boy who learned and grew like other boys, and that theology is not part of this book. What is fair to say now is that this little story of Jesus in the temple helped later Christians to avoid the idea, proposed by some, that Jesus was not truly human but only *appeared* to be human.

Before we leave this moment of encounter with Jesus, one other thing must be mentioned: there is a great deal to be learned from what is *not* here. That this is all we are given about his childhood and adolescence, by any of his biographers, leaves us with the near certainty that, at least in the worldly sense, his youthful years were normal. God did not just become one of us—he become an everyday one of us. This is what he wanted. This is what he chose. This fact should free us all from the notion that a life must be extraordinary in order to be full. Fullness is found in the ordinary, too.

Fanciful stories that he traveled to Japan or India, to Britain, or even to the Americas are sometimes proposed to fill in the blank years. But these proposals are worthless. Had these things happened, Mary would have known. Why would she later tell people, possibly Luke himself, about this one story of Jesus in the temple and hold back on a trip to India or Britain? Luke makes very clear that he is trying to tell us the true story of Jesus. Why would he leave such a detail out?

Even in the very early years of Christianity, in the writings of people who are sometimes called *Gnostics*, wild stories of Jesus as an almost wizard-like child of magical power were told. These, too, we can discount.

No, these fanciful stories are fictions. Any reasonable person will reject them. Jesus, born in Bethlehem and raised in Nazareth, lived an almost entirely uneventful life until he was about thirty years old. Mark's Gospel says he was a carpenter (or craftsman) and Matthew's says he was the son of a carpenter.

These memories of Jesus are not empty. They have had great importance down through time. Christians over the centuries have taken comfort in the fact that God, on becoming a man, worked with his hands. This emphasizes the great dignity of manual labor and promotes the interests of laborers. It is a beautiful tradition in Christianity, and one worth preserving against those who would turn Jesus into a world traveler or a seeker after the secrets of Eastern mystics.

He worked with his hands and lived a quiet life until he was about thirty. It was only then that he burst forth into public life and began the most remarkable three years any person has ever lived.

The Jews Prepare the World

The Jews made it possible for the world to understand and accept God when he came in person. In preparing the Jews, God prepared a reception delegation for himself. He prepared a people who could recognize him when he taught; he prepared scriptures and traditions that established a context in which people could interpret Jesus' strange teachings and actions.

Their role as God's chosen people made the Jews witnesses to God among the nations, but they also became the physical doorway through which God entered and interacted with the world. Their temple, their synagogues, and their other public spaces are the terrain of Jesus' ministry and the ministries of those he sent to share the good news.

These Jews shared their faith in the one God with others throughout the Roman world and as far away as India. And wherever they went, they built their synagogues to share God's revelation with many non-Jews. These friends of the Jews heard of the goodness, justice, oneness, and mercy of God and came to believe in him.

All of these people (perhaps numbered in the millions by the time of Jesus) were part of God's preparation of the world to accept his coming.

8

Our Third Moment with Jesus: "Follow Me"

To the left of the altar in the church of San Luigi dei Francesi in Rome hang three Caravaggio paintings, scenes from the life of Matthew the apostle.

The first shows Jesus calling Matthew to follow him. The second shows a much older Matthew writing his Gospel. And the third shows Matthew being killed for his witness to Jesus.

They are among the most beautiful objects in the world, but the first, the *Calling of St. Matthew*, is often thought to be Caravaggio's finest work. It is certainly one of the greatest paintings ever made.

Jesus is young and vibrant, but we see only the side of his face and his hand, which is extended, pointing at Matthew. The light comes from behind Jesus and shines directly into the face of Matthew, whose almost comical, almost heartbreaking expression suggests a complex emotional reaction to the call. He is at once astonished, uncertain, and deeply moved.

Peter, with his back to us, is whispering in the Messiah's ear and seems to be asking Jesus, "Are you sure about this?" Peter's hand also points at Matthew, but ambivalently, as if to say, "This is not our kind of people."

Jesus has no interest in Peter's concerns. His expression of serenity and gravity lets us know that his call of Matthew arises from depths within Jesus that none of the others in the room can fathom. Jesus, far wiser than they, knows exactly who he is calling, and nothing can move him to reconsider.

Here is the story as given in Matthew's Gospel:

> As Jesus passed on from there, he saw a man called Matthew sitting at the tax office; and he said to him, "Follow me." And he rose and followed him.
>
> And as he sat at table in the house, behold, many tax collectors and sinners came and sat down with Jesus and his disciples. And when the Pharisees saw this, they said to his disciples, "Why does your teacher eat with tax collectors and sinners?" But when he heard it, he said, "Those who are well have no need of a physician, but those who are sick. Go and learn what this means, 'I desire mercy, and not sacrifice.' For I came not to call the righteous, but sinners" (Matt. 9:9–13).

It is beyond doubt that Matthew knew who Jesus was well before Jesus looked at him and said, "Follow me." Everyone in the area was aware of the healing and preaching that Jesus was doing all around the Sea of Galilee. And Capernaum, where Matthew worked, was essentially the home base of Jesus' ministry.

Sitting each day in a public place, conducting public business, he would have heard the news almost as it happened. He would have met people who were sharing stories of the things Jesus said and did: a father telling of the sick child Jesus had healed, a prostitute re-living the moment Jesus had rebuked religious hypocrites.

But would Matthew have gone out with the crowds to see and hear Jesus for himself?

Likely, he would not.

However much his heart might have burned to meet Jesus, to see the miracles, to hear the preaching about the kingdom of God, Matthew seems to have thought such beautiful things were for others and not for himself.

Probably a multi-lingual and literate man, given his work as a tax collector, Matthew might have felt he did not belong among the great throngs of common people that Jesus seemed to love. What's more, Matthew was not a very good Jew. He was a collaborator with the Roman occupiers, which made him an enemy to his own people. What would the Messiah want with a man like him?

All around Matthew there was joy at the dawning of the kingdom of God, but he felt himself excluded. The kingdom, no matter how much he might want it, did not belong to him.

On the fateful day, as the crowds streamed past his customs post, Matthew would have known that Jesus was approaching, but he did not get up. He did not go out. Perhaps such a thing would have made him a fool in the eyes of the other officials. Perhaps it would have made him a target of his fellow Jews. Whatever was the case, Matthew suppressed the desires of his heart and did not move.

Certainly, he would have strained to see Jesus, maybe without letting others see him do it. Certainly, he would have hoped to hear a word or see a miracle as the Messiah passed. But he did nothing to make these hopes a reality. He remained seated even as Jesus approached.

Suddenly, he is there at the door. Why has he stopped? Why has he come to the customs post? The crowds wait to see. Matthew waits to see. Even now, Matthew does not know what is happening, until the eyes of the Messiah meet his own.

I indulge myself imagining the look on the face of Jesus, a wry smile that says, "You didn't think I'd come for you, but here I am."

With the words of Jesus, "Follow me," Matthew's entire world shifts. He sees now that he has not understood the kingdom of God at all.

The complications of his life did not mean that he had no place with the Messiah. His own moral failings had not excluded him. The joy of the kingdom was not just for the common people, the everyday Jews whom Jesus obviously loved. This love was for Matthew, as well.

Jesus paid a social cost at that moment, and Matthew would have been keenly aware of this. The crowds had seen

Jesus rebuke the unjust and would have sniggered as they prepared for Jesus to rebuke these customs-takers, these betrayer Jews. By calling Matthew, Jesus put himself at odds with the expectations of the crowd, knowing full well how quickly a crowd can become a mob.

Before his fellow tax collectors could mock him, before the crowd could turn against him, Matthew was on his feet and following. What haze of emotions must he have felt in that moment as he pursued Jesus down the main street of Capernaum, so vulnerable in the crowd, so amazed that this was really happening. Was the secret desire of his heart really being fulfilled?

Later, at dinner, how sheepish Matthew must have felt as the disciples of Jesus also paid a social cost for Matthew's presence. These good Jews, these common folk, found themselves abused by Pharisees and questioned about things they really had no answers for. *Why does your teacher eat with tax collectors and sinners?*

By calling Matthew, Jesus had opened the door to a whole new group. Now, in addition to good common Jews such as Peter, and the officious, educated Jews such as the Pharisees, a new group was gathered around Jesus: bad Jews—tax collectors and sinners. Everyone had to adjust to this new reality. We can easily imagine all the little dramas of resentment and social re-positioning that played out that evening.

This is where Matthew learned what kind of man Jesus was. Now he saw the heart of the one he had heard so much about. And it was just the opposite of what he probably expected from the Messiah. Wasn't the Messiah the one who would reward the righteous and restore them to their proper place? Wasn't he going to set things right so that the good people would get what they deserved? That's not at all the same as, "I came not to call the righteous, but sinners."

Why would Jesus prefer sinners over the righteous, even to the point of calling Matthew and dining with Matthew's friends, people who had persecuted some of the righteous people right there in the room? Jesus answers this when he tells the Pharisees, "Go and learn what this means, 'I desire mercy, and not sacrifice.'"

For Jesus, the word *righteousness* does not seem to mean merely rule-following. Somebody is not "righteous" just because he avoids doing overt evil. Rather, for Jesus, the meaning of the word seems to be rooted in the teachings of the Jewish prophets, who constantly called the people to generosity and mercy. For him, the desire for God within Matthew's heart is worth more than all the "righteous" deeds of the Pharisees. But, strangely, it is also worth more than the works of the good Jews and common folk who follow Jesus, such as Peter.

All the sacrifices that the Pharisees make, whether in the temple or in their daily lives, mean nothing without mercy in their hearts. The sacrifices do not make the person righteous; only mercy will. And this goes for the good Jews like Peter, as well. Just following the rules and living righteous lives does not make them righteous. They, too, need to have mercy on people such as Matthew and his friends.

Matthew is neither a noble Pharisee nor a common, salt-of-the-earth Jew. He does not presume to think the kingdom of God is for him. In fact, he figures he is excluded from it. But Jesus does not exclude him. No matter what the social cost, he calls Matthew to take a place right at the center of his messianic ministry.

Jesus calls himself a physician here, but he acts as a shepherd. He brings all the sheep together—Peter and his crowd, the Pharisees, and the tax collectors and sinners. If any of them want him, they must accept one another.

Jesus does not exclude anyone from following him. So long as the desire is there, Jesus says, "Follow me." He seeks out and finds the desiring heart, just as he found Matthew. And when he finds the desiring heart, he pulls that person close to him no matter what anyone else thinks, says, or does. He scandalizes both the good and the wicked with his mercy. He simply loves those who will accept his love, showing no preference for the good over the evil or the religious over the non-religious.

This is not to say he is satisfied to leave evildoers in their evil; nor does he leave the good to their own efforts. He calls everyone to what is truly good: fellowship with himself. He is the physician who makes them all well, if, like Matthew, they will just come with him when he calls.

As Caravaggio's second and third paintings make clear, Matthew's life is completely transformed by Jesus' willingness to ignore social pressures. His rock-solid willingness to pay any cost to share his table with those who desire his friendship makes it possible for Matthew to become the man who later writes a Gospel and accepts martyrdom.

The utter disregard for his own reputation reveals a fierceness in Jesus for people over image. He could have played the part of the Messiah, but he did not. He could simply have ignored Matthew and his friends. No one, not even Matthew, would have called him wrong to do so. But that is not Jesus. Jesus is the one who says, "Come to me, all who labor and are heavy laden, and I will give you rest. Take my yoke upon you, and learn from me; for I am gentle and lowly in heart, and you will find rest for your souls. For my yoke is easy, and my burden is light" (Matt. 11:28–30).

The Pagan World and Jesus

Beyond the special preparations God made for his own coming among the Jews, he also prepared the wider world. This world came to be called "pagan" by later Christians, who used the word primarily as an insult. Today it is used as a descriptive word rather than an insult; for a Christian, it means things such as nature religion, polytheism, ancestor worship, and even philosophical religions like Buddhism and Stoicism. Paganism represents all the attempts people make at connecting with the divine either before or apart from the revelation to the Jews.

God did not abandon this pagan world but put it through its own divine preparations so that it would be ready for the coming of Jesus. God's power permitted, and we can assume also fostered, Greek philosophy, Roman governance, and the vast "globalized" trade interconnections of Europe, Africa, and Asia that extended as far away as China. The *Pax Romana* that began just before the birth of Jesus and remained in effect for roughly 200 years after his death acted as a graced moment in which the Gospel could be preached to millions.

Without denying any of the cruelties of ancient governance, we see even in the New Testament how the systems of pagan governments assisted the growth of Christianity, most especially by maintaining a highly functioning civil society with a profound intellectual life.

The Roman cast of mind, with its great respect for ancient religions such as Judaism and its habits of rigorous philosophy modeled on the Greeks, was ready for the kinds of conversations needed if the gospel was to be intelligently accepted and spread.

The gospel certainly spread throughout the Roman Empire because it involved a new ethic of love and hope that appealed to the unloved and the hopeless. But it also spread—especially among the educated classes—because it was an intellectually satisfying faith. It explained the origins of the world, the nature of the divine, and the presence of evil in ways that satisfied, as nothing else could, the classically educated Roman mind.

When we perceive how God prepared both Jews and pagans, bestowing on them gifts that made it possible for the Good News to be understood and then to spread, we come to a further insight about who Jesus is: he is the center point of all human history. Long before he was born, the soil of history was being prepared for him. After he died and rose, that preparation allowed his message to flower within the soil of this world.

9

Our Fourth Moment with Jesus: A Disappointing Messiah

In the Acts of the Apostles, Luke describes the last moments that Jesus spent with his disciples before ascending into heaven:

> To them he presented himself alive after his passion by many proofs, appearing to them during forty days, and speaking of the kingdom of God. And while staying with them he charged them not to depart from Jerusalem, but to wait for the promise of the Father, which, he said, "you heard from me, for John baptized with water, but before many days you shall be baptized with the Holy Spirit." So when they had come together, they asked him, "Lord, will you at this time restore the kingdom to Israel?" He said to them, "It is not for you to know times or seasons which

the Father has fixed by his own authority. But you shall receive power when the Holy Spirit has come upon you; and you shall be my witnesses in Jerusalem and in all Judea and Samar'ia and to the end of the earth." And when he had said this, as they were looking on, he was lifted up, and a cloud took him out of their sight (Acts 1:3–9).

Here Jesus spends a profound moment with his closest followers. He has taught them for years, has done countless miracles, has died and has risen from the dead, and now is promising that they will shortly receive the Holy Spirit. But right in the middle of this important moment, they interrupt him to ask about when he will restore the kingdom to Israel. When will he be making himself king of Israel and replacing Rome with Israel as the world's ruler? After a curt reply to their interruption, Jesus goes right back to what he was saying about the Holy Spirit.

Why the disconnect? Why, after all this, are they still focused not on all he has done and is doing, but on something he has not done and that he shows no interest in doing?

What they mean when they ask if he is going, now, to restore the kingdom to Israel is whether he is going to take up the political and military rule of the world. They have been expecting him to do these things ever since they first came to believe that he was the Messiah. And what is more, they have been expecting, because they are his closest followers, to rule with him, to be officials of power within his new kingdom.

In this moment, we glimpse a burden that Jesus carried throughout his public life. Despite all he did, he was not what the people wanted him to be, even those closest to him.

He was a disappointing Messiah.

Certainly, Jesus had enemies who openly rejected him. And his enemies made his life difficult. But his relationship with those who loved him, because they never stopped imposing worldly expectations on him, added greatly to his difficulties. They rejected him, too, in their own way, by refusing to meet him as he was.

They clung to their desire for how the Messiah *should* be instead of loving the Messiah as he was. Even knowing him to be unlike anyone they had ever met, they did not adjust their expectations. Even living each day with his gentleness, his kindness, his tireless patience, they did not shift their image of the Messiah. As they followed him, they simply waited for the day when he would turn into the worldly and commanding Messiah they were expecting—one who would rule rather than one who would serve.

How alone this made him. His own friends, those he most loved, looked right past him and saw only what they wanted to see. They knew he had power. They had seen him walking on water and controlling the weather. It never occurred to them that he would not use power in a human way—to break the Roman hold on the world and establish a renewed kingdom of Israel.

Instead, he used his power only in a divinely humble way—to love people and save them from sin and death.

He spent his life revealing to them that God was not what they thought, and they never quite got it. To them, God's rule would be like any king's rule. He would force the world to conform to his will. For Jesus, God's rule is not imposed but is offered as an invitation. It depends on persuasion, not on coercion.

We cannot get to know Jesus without grasping his aloneness in this world. He was light and life, but "men loved darkness rather than light, because their deeds were evil" (John 3:19). His enemies openly spoke about their fear of him. After one of his miracles, reports got back to the religious authorities, men who maintained their power by avoiding trouble with Rome. They asked themselves, "What are we to do? For this man performs many signs. If we let him go on thus, everyone will believe in him, and the Romans will come and destroy both our holy place and our nation" (John 11:47–48).

People also quite publicly erupted in anger at him. For example, on one occasion when Jesus scolded the local people for their unbelief, "all in the synagogue were filled with wrath. And they rose up and put him out of the city, and led him to the brow of the hill on which their city was built, that they might throw him down headlong" (Luke 4:28–29).

And all the while his followers anticipated that he would eventually show himself as the kind of Messiah who could crush these enemies and take command of Israel and the world; the type of Messiah they had been taught all their lives to expect. Hoping for offices of power in the renewed kingdom of Israel, his disciples did not see that Jesus was offering them offices of a different kind. The power he would give them would be the power of the Holy Spirit—the power to love freely. They would be not commanders but witnesses. Their role would not be to control and command but to invite and persuade.

So Jesus has to lead them toward a higher form of hope. He cannot conform to their hopes because their hopes are for a kind of salvation that will not last. He wants them to have what will last forever—joy and freedom of spirit; love and intimacy with God, who is pure love.

He lived not to force the world to conform to God's will, but to reveal the true nature of God: humble, loving, infinitely generous and patient. He did not come to be just another great man, not even the greatest man, if what we understand by "greatness" is the exercise of power over others. Rather, he healed, he encouraged, and he taught—inviting people to join him in healing, encouraging, and teaching.

In living this way, he showed what God is really like. This is the cause of his alone-ness in this life. Only he knows what God is really like. Everyone else has an image of God; everyone else has an image of God's Messiah. And none of these images is correct. For this reason, Jesus has to live and act in ways that are strange, incomprehensible. He has to suffer being misunderstood so that people can be freed from images and unreality and come to see, in him, what reality is really like, what God is really like. He was "the image of the invisible God" (Col. 1:15).

What Jesus reveals about God makes it clear that God's plan is not just to remove the evil from power and to replace their power with his own. Rather, his plan is to invite people into a much deeper kind of power—the power to love one another, and to be free from all the sins that mar love. God's plan is to make friends and to share with his friends everything he has. Those who have done evil are just as welcome as those who have done good. Those with power are just as welcome as the powerless.

We do not always like this fact—that the evil and the good are equally welcome in the kingdom of God. We don't want him to give himself to the evildoers; we want him to triumph over them. A great deal about Jesus can be understood if we understand that he came to call everyone—both the good and the evil—to repentance. Everyone must change in order to receive the kingdom of God as Jesus offers it.

There is no more perfect example of this than the longest story Jesus ever told, and one of his most famous: the parable of the prodigal son.

In this parable, a loving father has two sons, one who we would call a good son and one who we would call a bad son. The good son is dutiful and does all that his father asks. The bad son—the prodigal—is selfish. He takes his inheritance and abandons his home to go off seeking pleasure.

The good son prospers at home with his father. The bad son loses everything and has to return home to his father in humiliation, hoping to be put to work as a hired hand. When the father sees the bad son coming home, he rushes out to meet him and treats him with a lavish outpouring of love.

In this we have a beautiful image of God the Father, of course, and his desire to have his wayward children home with him. Most teachers would have ended their story here.

But not Jesus.

He goes on to tell of the resentment of the good son who wants his bad brother punished. This son wants credit for all the good he has done, and he wants his brother to bear the full force of his guilt.

The good son is operating on the law of karma, the law of justice, the principle that says what goes around comes around and everyone should get what he deserves. It does not matter how "good" the good brother is; his heart is still dead because he does not love his brother (or his father) truly. He just wants to do good and get what he believes he deserves.

Both the bad son *and* the good son must repent if they are to have what is best for them: a relationship of love with their father and with each other.

In the Gospels, Jesus is exactly like that father. He calls everyone to repent—both the bad and the good. Everyone must turn from what he is doing, from his own opinions of how things should be, his own demands on reality, and accept the love of the Father that is given freely. Both the bad and the good must accept that we have been poor brothers and sisters to each other because we have not really loved our Father or each other.

Like the father in the parable who was not understood or truly loved by either of his sons, Jesus lived a life of intense alone-ness even while he patiently offered a life of intimate togetherness. "I have come down from heaven, not to do my own will, but the will of him who sent me," Jesus tells the crowd in John's Gospel (6:37–38). And not long after, in the face of being rejected by the scholars, he says, "And he who sent me is with me; he has not left me alone, for I always do what is pleasing to him" (John 8:29).

Earlier, John has told us directly what the will of God is for Jesus: "For God sent the Son into the world, not to condemn the world, but that the world might be saved through him" (John 3:17). In hoping for a political and military Messiah, the followers of Jesus were committing themselves to a hope that was too small. Hoping for the kind of victory that merely shifts who rules this world is, ultimately, no hope at all. It does not get to the root of the problem—that the human family is shattered.

In disappointing their hopes, Jesus reveals God's higher plan, rooted in a loving Father's desire to put the human family back together—the good and the bad, the worthy and the wicked—so that everyone can be loved.

"News" About Jesus

The followers of Jesus went about sharing the news that Jesus was God and had risen from the dead. The question is, was this news true?

We tend to trust news when a) we trust those who bring the news and/or b) when the news itself rings true. In the case of Jesus' resurrection, those who bring the news—his apostles and disciples—come across as eminently trustworthy. Their manner of witness, their manner of life, and everything else about them suggests that these were serious men and women with clear minds and good hearts who desired to faithfully transmit news about real events. Likewise their steadfast belief in the truth of the news despite it resulting in their persecution.

But, as trustworthy as those who shared the news of the Resurrection seem, does the news itself ring true? Is it plausible that Jesus could have risen from the dead?

The answer to this question, of course, is related to our general willingness to believe in miracles. If we are dead set against them, then no, we cannot credit the Resurrection. But there is no logical reason why a modern person should be against miracles. The idea that God could intervene in time and space is not in conflict with any modern understanding of time or space. Even if we are devout in our adherence to modern science, we must admit that the Resurrection *could have happened.*

There are other books that assemble the evidence for the Resurrection, and this is not the place to review all that evidence, but consider just this, a fact often noted by scholar Gary Habermas: James the kinsman of Jesus and Paul the apostle both lived and died saying that they had seen him alive after death. They did not claim that they believed he was raised, but that they had met him and spoken with him. This is surprising because neither of these men accepted Jesus or his claims before his death. Both claimed—and we have multiple sources for their claims—that they met Jesus alive after his death and began to follow him.

Couple this with the fact that, as modern New Testament scholars tell us, virtually no time elapsed (probably days, maybe weeks or months) between the time Jesus died and the time early Christians began going out to tell the world that he was raised, and we have to ask ourselves, what happened to cause this sudden conviction among many people, including some who refused to follow Jesus before his death, that they had seen him alive? And how were they able to make this claim when anyone could have gone a few yards outside Jerusalem to check Jesus' tomb?

Again, there are mountains of other evidence for the resurrection of Jesus, but I focus just on the sudden conversions of James and Paul, and the sudden burst of proclamation that Jesus was alive, for this reason: such little details ring true. And there are lots of these little details, many from three, four, or five different sources, that, taken together, become quite convincing. This event happened; no other explanation quite fits with the details.

Moreover, and here I speak only for myself, it all rings true as something God would do. It is all surprising but somehow also fitting. One does not expect it, but now that it has happened, one finds it compellingly consistent—and spiritually satisfying.

It makes sense that God would not leave us alone but would come in search of us like a shepherd in search of lost sheep.

It makes sense that God would restore friendship to us in a way that is meek, and kind, and patient—even patient unto death.

It makes sense that God would not overpower us or force us to follow him into this new life of love, but that he would simply invite us and let us choose for ourselves.

Yes, this is how God would live among his people: not as a ruler but a servant, not as a taskmaster but as a healer, not as one for himself but as one for others.

By dying on a cross to satisfy justice in our place, and by rising from the dead and sending others to share news of him, Jesus presents the love of God in a way that can draw all people to himself, while, at the same time, leaving everyone free to accept or reject him without being in any way coerced or compelled. This story, this news, taken as a whole and given to us by people who seem in every way honest and noble, rings quite true.

10

Our Fifth Moment with Jesus: A Teacher of Strange Things

At some points in John's Gospel, Jesus seems to be speaking in a state of ecstasy, almost as if he is half in this world and half in a higher world. It is as if he is, at the same time, seeing all those in front of him and being drawn up into some higher vision that only he can see.

This baffles everyone around him. For John, Jesus is a light so bright that his center point is hard to see. Even those who want to are unable to look directly at him; they need help.

John knew Jesus well, and we can be sure that his image of Jesus as a person shining overwhelmingly brightly is a true recollection. As much as Jesus was charismatic and sociable, welcoming and friendly, he was also strange and at times disturbing. Even when you adjusted to him, you could be sure that you'd soon have to adjust again. He kept surprising.

This must have felt demanding, sometimes even frightening, to those who followed him most closely: his little church of seventy or so closest friends. Nowhere is the strange otherworldliness of Jesus more apparent than in the sixth chapter of John's Gospel.

A huge crowd is following Jesus because he has just performed the miracle of feeding thousands of people by multiplying a few loaves of bread and some fish. This is the moment when they decide to make him king, so certain are they that he is the Messiah and filled with power.

Jesus refuses their adulation and seems almost to insult them: "You are looking for me not because you saw signs but because you ate the loaves and were filled" (John 6:26). There is a back-and-forth nature to his conversation with the crowd that makes it seem more agitated than most of Jesus' conversations. He is not just teaching them; he is engaging in a vigorous dispute with them. And what he has to say shocks them.

I give it to you here in full in order to convey the true strangeness of Jesus. If we take him to be a wise and good teacher, we must admit that here he comes across almost as deranged, so far is he pushing the boundaries of normal speech:

> Jesus said to them, "I am the bread of life; he who comes to me shall not hunger, and he who believes in me shall never thirst. But I said to you that you have seen me and yet do not believe. All that the Father gives me will come to me; and him who comes to me I will not cast out. For

I have come down from heaven, not to do my own will, but the will of him who sent me; and this is the will of him who sent me, that I should lose nothing of all that he has given me, but raise it up at the last day. For this is the will of my Father, that everyone who sees the Son and believes in him should have eternal life; and I will raise him up at the last day."

The Jews then murmured at him, because he said, "I am the bread which came down from heaven." They said, "Is not this Jesus, the son of Joseph, whose father and mother we know? How does he now say, 'I have come down from heaven'?"

Jesus answered them, "Do not murmur among yourselves. No one can come to me unless the Father who sent me draws him; and I will raise him up at the last day. It is written in the prophets, 'And they shall all be taught by God.' Everyone who has heard and learned from the Father comes to me. Not that anyone has seen the Father except him who is from God; he has seen the Father. Truly, truly, I say to you, he who believes has eternal life. I am the bread of life. Your fathers ate the manna in the wilderness, and they died. This is the bread which comes down from heaven, that a man may eat of it and not die. I am the living bread which came down from heaven; if anyone eats of this bread, he will live forever; and the bread which I shall give for the life of the world is my flesh."

The Jews then disputed among themselves, saying, "How can this man give us his flesh to eat?" So Jesus said to them, "Truly, truly, I say to you, unless you eat the flesh of the Son of man and drink his blood, you have no life in you; he who eats my flesh and drinks my blood has eternal life, and I will raise him up at the last day. For my flesh is food indeed, and my blood is drink indeed. He who eats my flesh and drinks my blood abides in me, and I in him. As the living Father sent me, and I live because of the Father, so he who eats me will live because of me. This is the bread which came down from heaven, not such as the fathers ate and died; he who eats this bread will live forever." This he said in the synagogue, as he taught at Caper'na-um.

Many of his disciples, when they heard it, said, "This is a hard saying; who can listen to it?" But Jesus, knowing in himself that his disciples murmured at it, said to them, "Do you take offense at this? Then what if you were to see the Son of man ascending where he was before? It is the spirit that gives life, the flesh is of no avail; the words that I have spoken to you are spirit and life. But there are some of you that do not believe." For Jesus knew from the first who those were that did not believe, and who it was that should betray him. And he said, "This is why I told you that no one can come to me unless it is granted him by the Father."

After this many of his disciples drew back and no longer went about with him. Jesus said to the twelve, "Will you also go away?" Simon Peter answered him, "Lord, to whom shall we go? You have the words of eternal life;

and we have believed, and have come to know, that you are the Holy One of God" (John 6:35–69).

Here Peter, as he so often does, speaks for the group. He does not assure Jesus that they understand him, only that they are not leaving him. Unlike the crowd, this small group follows Jesus because of who Jesus is, not because of what he can do. They have gotten to know him, and they have entrusted themselves to him.

Having done so, they have nowhere else to go. But just like everyone else, including Jesus himself, they are aware that he has just said some very strange and upsetting things. The moment is raw and unnerving. Jesus has just told thousands of people that unless they eat him and drink him, they will not have life. He has told them that his flesh is true food and his blood is true drink.

If any other person had said such things, he would be dismissed as crazy. But Jesus is not crazy, and the apostles know it. Something far stranger than madness is going on. They are being led out of the everyday world into places they do not understand. Only the fact that they have come to love Jesus and trust him keeps them with him now, at this alarming moment.

What they cannot know at this moment is that Jesus is going to die. He is going to lie in a tomb. And then he is going to rise to new life. His risen flesh will have qualities that normal flesh does not have—qualities that make it able to do things that are mysterious to us.

As Paul writes, "It is sown a physical body, it is raised a spiritual body" (1 Cor. 15:44). Now, everywhere the scriptures make clear that Jesus was resurrected bodily. But Paul does say that the risen body of Jesus is a "spiritual body." That is to say, the risen body of Jesus is no longer subject to the weaknesses, the corruption, the vulnerabilities, and the limitations of earthly flesh. Like a spirit, it is immortal and unbound from the usual physical laws. The risen body of Jesus can do things that we normally would associate only with spirits—like passing through walls, as Jesus does after the Resurrection.

It is this risen flesh and blood that they are to consume. The risen body of Jesus can be shared as food, real food, and this food can share with those who eat it everything that Jesus is. It can be shared in the way a spirit can be shared, though it is not a spirit but a body.

In the Bread of Life discourse, Jesus does not explain *how* his followers are to consume his body and blood, only that they must. Only later, at the Last Supper, does he show them how this is to happen:

> The Lord Jesus on the night when he was betrayed took bread, and when he had given thanks, he broke it, and said, "This is my body which is for you. Do this in remembrance of me." In the same way also the cup, after supper, saying, "This cup is the new covenant in my blood. Do this, as often as you drink it, in remembrance of me" (1 Cor. 11:23–25).

Paul then adds, "Whoever, therefore, eats the bread or drinks the cup of the Lord in an unworthy manner will be guilty of profaning the body and blood of the Lord" (1 Cor. 11:28).

Here, Paul is writing down words that the earliest Christians heard repeated every Sunday when they gathered for the memorial meal as Jesus had commanded. The risen Jesus shared his real—but mysteriously transformed—flesh and blood with them at these meals.

This is the religion that the apostles taught, a religion of intimacy with God by sharing in the body and blood of the risen Son of God. And just as Jesus had to use forceful language to make clear that his very strange teaching was received in all its shocking power, so here we see Paul having to use forceful language, warning people that this *really is* the body and blood of the Lord, and they will have to answer for it if they receive it unworthily.

Following the example of Jesus and the apostles, the bishops and teachers of the early Church also resorted to harsh language to make clear to people how serious this teaching of Jesus is—that eating his real body and drinking his real blood is the only way to eternal life.

For example, the bishop and martyr Ignatius of Antioch, a man who knew John and was intimately familiar with John's Gospel both in writing and from John's mouth, warned (in letters he wrote just eighty years after Jesus died) against false teachers who "do not confess that the Eucharist is the flesh of our Savior Jesus Christ, flesh which suffered for our sins and which that Father, in his goodness, raised up again."[1]

1 Epistle to the Smyrnaeans

He told his fellow Christians, "I have no taste for corruptible food nor for the pleasures of this life. I desire the bread of God, which is the flesh of Jesus Christ, who was of the seed of David; and for drink I desire his blood, which is love incorruptible."[2]

Even today, many followers of Jesus refuse to follow him into the depths of this strange teaching. They try to tame this "hard" teaching of Jesus by taking away its strangeness and making it symbolic or metaphorical. Yet neither the apostles nor the earliest Christians, nor Jesus himself, gave any indication that this teaching is anything but shocking in its bluntness: either we eat his flesh and drink his blood, or we do not share in his life.

If we want an answer to what Jesus was like, we have to accept this, too: he is strange. He says and does things that, even after 2,000 years of reflection and consideration, still force us into depths of reality that are far beyond the world as we usually experience it.

When we encounter the strangeness of Jesus, we can walk away or dismiss him as a madman just as the crowd did. Or we can trust him and follow him into the depths where, in time, all will become clear.

Peter himself followed him into the depths and must have meditated on these things many times, asking himself why it all had to be so strange, why Jesus seemed to demand that people follow him even when they struggled to understand him.

2   Epistle to the Romans

Peter shared his conclusion in his second letter when he told his fellow Christians that Jesus "has granted to us his precious and very great promises, that through these you may escape from the corruption that is in the world because of passion, and become partakers of the divine nature" (2 Pet. 1:3–4).

These words come in a letter that was written very late in Peter's life and may even have been written after Peter's death by an author communicating things that Peter had taught. Here, at the end of his life, Peter sees clearly what all of this is about—and why it has been so strange. Jesus intends for human beings not only to live with God in heaven, but to "become partakers of the divine nature." Christian life reaches its final goal when the Christian person becomes like God and participates in his life.

This is why Jesus leads his disciples into strange and demanding truths—so we can see the strangest and most demanding truth of all. The deepest good of the good news is that, somehow, we shall be like God.

This cannot happen in safety. It cannot happen in comfort. To be so transformed that we may share in the divine nature, we must move out from safety into a great and dangerous adventure. We must let go of comfort and allow ourselves to be transformed by divine and angelic powers so far above us as to be incomprehensible.

Peter stepped out of the boat to walk on the water with Jesus. Every Christian must do likewise. This is the strangeness of Jesus and of the life he offers. It is life in full, and it takes every virtue, not least of all courage, to follow him.

Jesus and Apocalyptic Messianism

As we have seen, Jesus began his public ministry by proclaiming, "This is the time of fulfillment. The kingdom of God is at hand. Repent, and believe in the good news." Modern scholars often ponder how a Jewish person at the time of Jesus would have understood this preaching. What would those words have meant in context?

In part, this is a hopeless task. The words are mysterious, and no amount of investigation into the ancient mindset can relieve them of their essential mystery. These words represent God calling out to his children, and his call is rich and multilayered. But the context provided by modern scholarship does suggest that Jesus' words are related to the state of religious agitation and excitement that was alive among the Jews of his time.

Just forty years after Jesus, this agitated religious state—often referred to as *messianic apocalypticism*—would lead to disaster, as those living in the Holy Land attempted a religious war against the Romans. This war resulted in the death of hundreds of thousands and the destruction of the temple in Jerusalem.

Part of Jesus' task as a teacher, leader, and religious founder was to mold the people's expectations and lead them away from ideas of immediate political revolution. His was to be a different kind of movement, one that involved not just a change to the political structures of the world but salvation from sin and death. When we see how often he is misunderstood, even by his own followers, we get a sense of how hard the job was of getting people to re-imagine the meaning of the coming of the Messiah.

11

Our Sixth Moment with Jesus: Friendship with God

Many people think of Jesus primarily as a teacher of morals: someone who shows us the good and right way to live. But this way of thinking about Jesus can easily miss the point of what Jesus truly taught.

He *does* teach morals, yes, and his moral teaching can be hard. Consider just a few of his admonitions from the Sermon on the Mount in the fifth chapter of Matthew's Gospel:

You have heard that it was said to the men of old, "You shall not kill; and whoever kills shall be liable to judgment." But I say to you that everyone who is angry with his brother shall be liable to judgment; whoever insults his brother shall be liable to the council, and whoever says, "You fool!" shall be liable to the hell of fire (Matt. 5:21–22).

You have heard that it was said, "You shall not commit adultery." But I say to you that everyone who looks at a woman lustfully has already committed adultery with her in his heart (Matt. 5:27–28).

It was also said, "Whoever divorces his wife, let him give her a certificate of divorce." But I say to you that everyone who divorces his wife, except on the ground of unchastity, makes her an adulteress; and whoever marries a divorced woman commits adultery (Matt. 5:31–32).

You have heard that it was said, "An eye for an eye and a tooth for a tooth." But I say to you, Do not resist one who is evil. But if anyone strikes you on the right cheek, turn to him the other also; and if anyone would sue you and take your coat, let him have your cloak as well; and if anyone forces you to go one mile, go with him two miles. Give to him who begs from you, and do not refuse him who would borrow from you (Matt. 5:38–42).

And, just in case none of those is hard enough for you, there is also this: "You have heard that it was said, 'You shall love your neighbor and hate your enemy.' But I say to you, Love your enemies and pray for those who persecute you" (Matt. 5:43–44).

But although such moral commands form an important element of what Jesus taught, they only show their full value within a larger whole. For what Jesus teaches, primarily, is *friendship with God.* And the kind of friendship Jesus teaches is so intimate that it can be called *communion,* a shared life of love.

Moral instruction, with Jesus, is always instruction in how to live as a friend of God, to remain in the peace and joy of communion with our Father in heaven. In this, he draws deeply on the Jewish faith. For example, when Jesus is asked by an honest Jewish teacher about which is the most important commandment, he answers as any good Jew would. Taking his text from the Torah, Jesus says,

> The first is, "Hear, O Israel: The Lord our God, the Lord is one; and you shall love the Lord your God with all your heart, and with all your soul, and with all your mind, and with all your strength." The second is this, "You shall love your neighbor as yourself." There is no other commandment greater than these (Mark 12:29–31).

For the Jews, a relationship of love of God was the center of everything. And God, as he told the prophet Jeremiah, loves his people with an everlasting love. For this reason, the love of God, if it is to be genuine, must extend to people. These relationships of love—with God and neighbor—form the basis for Jewish morality, and Jesus unbreakably aligns himself with this order of things.

Jesus wants his follower to be caught up into a love life with God, and he wants to remove every obstacle to that life. Recall how he scolds the Pharisees when they objected to his eating with Matthew and the other sinners. Jesus does not say, "Lighten up; it is okay to be a sinner." He does not deny the Pharisees their authority as teachers of morality, even telling people at one point, "The scribes and the Pharisees sit on Moses' seat; so practice and observe whatever they tell you" (Matt. 23:2–3).

What is more, as we have seen, Jesus repeatedly commands people to give up sin and instructs them about what things are sinful. No, Jesus does not object to morality. His objection to the Pharisees is that their morality is disconnected from mercy, the highest form of love. Morality divorced from love is false religion.

Let us spend one last moment with Jesus, then.

Just before he goes to die, Jesus speaks openly and passionately with his closest friends about what he wants for them:

As the Father has loved me, so have I loved you; abide in my love. If you keep my commandments, you will abide in my love, just as I have kept my Father's commandments and abide in his love. These things I have spoken to you, that my joy may be in you, and that your joy may be full.

This is my commandment, that you love one another as I have loved you. Greater love has no man than this, that a man lay down his life for his friends. You are my friends if you do what I command you. No longer do I call you servants, for the servant does not know what his master is doing; but I have called you friends, for all that I have heard from my Father I have made known to you. You did not choose me, but I chose you and appointed you that you should go and bear fruit and that your fruit should abide; so that whatever you ask the Father in my name, he may give it to you. This I command you, to love one another" (John 15:9–17).

The commandment to "love one another as I have loved you," which is re-emphasized with the final, emphatic order to "love one another," is the hardest commandment he ever gives. There is no question what it means because it is given as he is preparing to suffer and die for them. The commandment to "love one another as I have loved you" is a commandment to surrender absolutely to the good of others, to donate oneself entirely to others for their good—just as he is preparing to do.

Something deep within us recoils at this. *I will lose everything if I am poured out for others.* It can be horrifying to imagine just how much Jesus is asking here. And the modern world, with its philosophies of self-empowerment, self-promotion, and self-help cannot see such self-giving love as anything other than abusive.

In the modern world, people are encouraged constantly to get what is theirs—whether it is respect or money or attention or pleasure. This world simply cannot understand self-giving love as anything other than an abuse of rights, an abuse of self-care.

But it is not abusive, and Jesus explains why when he puts this commandment into the context of divine love. He says his Father loves him. That is to say, his Father completely *donates himself* to Jesus, his Son. When Jesus says, "I have kept my Father's commandments, and abide in his love" (John

15:10), he is not just saying, "I'm a good boy who never breaks the rules." He is saying that he does what the Father does: he donates himself in love back to the Father.

The Father gives himself to the Son in love, and this love comes with a commandment: that the Son give himself in love. This commandment is not bossiness. It is not, "Do this or else." It is a commandment of love, given not to bend the will of another but rather so that the sharing of love—freely given and freely received—can continue.

Think of the parent who commands the child learning to play ball, "Throw it back to me." By throwing the ball to the child, the parent has initiated a game; the loving command to throw it back is a call for the child to share in the game; then the two will be playing together.

Or consider a slightly better analogy: a parent with two children. In love he throws the ball to one child, and in love he commands, "Now throw it to your sister, and she will throw it back to me." The child participates in the game by following the command of love to include everyone in the game. This is how the child who receives the ball loves and obeys the parent, by including the sister. Then all three are joined in a shared undertaking. They are all participating together in something that brings all of them joy.

That is why Jesus, upon inviting the disciples into this divine game, tells them, "These things I have spoken to you, that my joy may be in you, and that your joy may be full" (John 15:11).

Joy can only be received if we enter into the great sharing of love that is God—Father, Son, and Holy Spirit—and our entry point is Jesus, who is God come down as a man for the purpose of bringing us up into the infinitely loving life of the divine. The only true Son of God becomes our brother so that we can be incorporated into the family and made adopted sons and daughters of God.

As Paul says to the earliest Christians, "Though he was rich, yet for your sake he became poor, so that by his poverty you might become rich" (2 Cor. 8:9).

"You are my friends if you do what I command you" (John 15:14) stands out here as the key to understanding Jesus as a moral teacher. His command is that they love others as he has loved them. He has included them in the sharing of divine love, and such love must extend to all of God's children. We cannot love God and refuse to toss the ball of love to our brother or sister.

All of his teaching against anger, greed, lust, divorce, and even grudges against enemies, is meant to dispose us to live for the good of others, to make our own life, like his life, into a gift for the joy of others.

In this way we are able to receive the fullness of the love of God by participating in the divine exchange of love that, like a game of catch, must be shared if it is to be received. The presence of divine love, and our participation in it, is the life of joy. Likewise, all of his commands—that we visit prisoners, feed the hungry, and generally do for others as we would have done for ourselves—are commands meant to widen the circle of love until none are left out.

He does not ask his followers to do these things on their own. He tells them that the Father, who sent him, will also send the

Holy Spirit to dwell within them, once Jesus has returned to the Father. Jesus has gained for them the right to be called sons and daughters of God; the Holy Spirit will give them the power to live as sons and daughters of God because the Spirit has the power to fulfill God's ancient promise to remove their hearts of stone and give them hearts of flesh (Ezek. 36:26).

And it happened. The Holy Spirit did descend upon them, they changed, and they changed the world.

All of this happened in the first century A.D., and in a sense it didn't meet its greatest challenge for nineteen hundred years—with the dawn of mass media and the sexual revolution, in which the Christian dynamic of free love became tied up with an ethic of sexual exploitation that went by the same name. This sexual revolution reversed the logic of friendship with God as Jesus taught it.

It might seem out of place here suddenly to leave Jesus and the apostles and fast-forward to the sexual revolution, but it's apt. Instead of living the difficult and transforming morality of Jesus, rooted in love of God and the desire to love others without cost, modern people began to think of morality as an obstacle to "love"—which they defined as the fulfillment of their sexual wants. They abandoned the self-control taught by Jesus, a self-control that makes us loving servants of others. In its place they embraced the search for fulfillment through the abandonment of self-control in favor of the false freedom of doing as we pleased.

Friendship with Jesus is not about doing as we please, but about following the Father's way of love: a love that lives for others and not merely for ourselves.

Instead of learning self-control, as Jesus taught, so that we could "remain" in the love of Jesus and the Father and be free from selfishness, the "free love" of the sexual revolution allowed people to use each other selfishly, to experience each other intimately without really giving themselves fully and permanently.

Once adopted, this sexual ethic extends to every other area of life. People become preoccupied with themselves. They become impatient and demanding. They value the pleasures of the flesh more than the joys of the spirit. This makes them not happy and peaceful but restless, agitated, angry, suspicious, and demanding. And the primary victims of this society of selfish "love" are those who have the hardest time looking out for themselves—the very old, the very young, and the otherwise vulnerable.

This distorted view of love, pervasive in our media age, is the number-one obstacle to spreading the love of Jesus. People who have become accustomed to an ethic of "free love" as a kind of holiday from morality find this way of life (unfulfilling though it is) very hard to give up. They mock those who still cling to the morality of Jesus as backward and even childish.

For such people—most of us modern people, most of the time—it is hard to accept friendship with Jesus because the fullness of friendship comes with this: "You are my friends if you do what I command you" (John 15:14).

But in the light of what Jesus is teaching, here, about divine love as the cause of joy, we see that his commandments are no threat at all to full and mature human happiness—they are the doorway to it. In our hearts, we desperately need and desire friendship with God, who is all goodness, truth, beauty, and kindness. Jesus shows us that the dynamics of this friendship are simple: receive what the Father gives freely, and then give ourselves freely to others.

If you do not know what it means to give yourself freely to others, Jesus is the model. Most people know the story of Jesus washing the feet of his disciples, a task normally reserved for a slave. His words as he washed their feet tell us with certainty where to look if we are not sure what true love looks like: "I have given you an example, that you also should do as I have done to you" (John 13:15).

Left on our own, we cast about looking for love, breaking hearts and having our hearts broken. But in friendship with Jesus, we are not alone, and our hearts will not be broken. In Jesus, God has offered us intimate friendship. If we follow his commandments, the joy of that friendship will remain with us forever.

The Historical Record of Jesus

One reason people give for refusing to put their faith in Jesus is that they lack confidence in the ancient sources. They are not convinced, they say, that these sources are reliable enough to establish a solid foundation of facts about Jesus.

This lack of trust in the ancient sources cannot be because there are too few of them. Within a lifetime of Jesus, there are scores of independent sources for him—an extraordinary number for an ordinary person of the ancient world.

The lack of trust also cannot be because the manuscripts of our sources for Jesus are unreliable. Manuscripts about Jesus can be dated earlier by hundreds of years than most ancient works, including major works that no one mistrusts, such as Caesar's *Commentaries* or Cicero's *De Re Publica*.

So, if we have plenty of ancient sources about Jesus and if the historical record of those sources is of high quality, why the lack of trust? One of the features of the modern personality, I think, is that we tend to dismiss pre-modern people as backward or superstitious. After all, we reason, they were less developed than we are, and their world was full of magical thinking.

So, when people say they do not trust the Gospels and the letters of the New Testament, they are, in truth, saying that they do not trust the people who wrote them.

Part of this distrust of ancient people is connected to our ignorance of them. How many ancient texts are taught in school anymore? How much of the philosophy or daily life of ancient people are we moderns exposed to? So it's fair to say that a good part of why we don't trust them is that we don't *know* them.

But another part of our distrust of ancient people is rooted in something we believe about ourselves: that we alone live in an enlightened time, the time of science and reason, and so we are wiser and more connected to the truth than any other people before us. And why should we believe people who lived in time of myth if we live in a time of science and reason?

In fact, the New Testament writers were quite conscious of the power of myth, and they explicitly taught against believing in myths. Peter himself stressed this point, "For we did not follow cleverly devised myths when we made known to you the power and coming of our Lord Jesus Christ, but we were eyewitnesses" (2 Pet. 1:16).

In fact, the New Testament is, in many respects, written to challenge mythological and superstitious thinking. Jesus himself was a startlingly practical teacher who told people such things as "the truth will make you free" (John 8:32).

The apostle Paul, in instructing one of the first bishops of the new Church, exhorted him, "Have nothing to do with godless and silly myths. Train yourself in godliness" (1 Tim. 4:7).

Peter exhorted new Christians to "gird up your minds, be sober" (1 Pet. 1:13).

All of this is consistent with a broad body of New Testament teaching against spiritual showmanship, sorcery, fortune-telling, and every kind of deception.

Far from being backward because they are ancient, the people who gave us the New Testament were trailblazers who made it possible for the world to rise above myth and superstition. We often forget it now, but more than a thousand years of Christian schools, monasteries, and universities provided the foundations for the modern world. If we dismiss the ancient writers of Scripture as unreasoned people, we dismiss the very roots of our own era's dedication to truth and reason.

12

Jesus on the Cross

We cannot finish this section of the book without asking a very basic question: why did Jesus die on the cross?

Of course, we can say he did so because he was sentenced to death by a Roman procurator. But as God, he could have avoided that death sentence or kept it from being carried out. So that does not fully explain it.

In another sense, he did so to fulfill centuries of messianic prophecy. But, again, he was the author of those prophecies, and he could have prevented them. Why didn't he? Why, in fact, did he *embrace* such a death? "No one takes [my life] from me, but I lay it down of my own accord," he said (John 10:17–18).

What is the point of the Son of God becoming man and then being rejected, tortured, and executed?

Perhaps the easiest biblical explanation for the death of Jesus on the cross comes from John the Baptist, who calls Jesus the "Lamb of God who takes away the sins of the world" (John 1:29). This statement connects Jesus to the Jewish feast of Passover, in which lambs were offered as sacrifices to God and then eaten, in commemoration of when God led the Jews out of slavery in Egypt (Exod. 12).

In this way of thinking, Jesus died as a lamb of sacrifice to take away the sins of the world. This answer also fits with the central religious practice of historical Christianity: the practice of eating his flesh.

The logic of religious sacrifice is complex, but certainly the Passover sacrifice of the lamb involves an exchange of gifts between God and his people. God has given the lamb. In sacrificing the lamb, his people give it back to him. This exchange of gifts draws them together, as all exchanges of gifts draw people together. And in eating the Lamb that has been offered to God, they, essentially, share a meal with God, a thing of great intimacy that represents a sharing of life, a relationship of closeness, between God and the people.

Calling Jesus the "Lamb of God," John the Baptist draws on the image of the Passover lamb to explain the meaning of Jesus. God has given Jesus, like a lamb, to humanity. On behalf of humanity, Jesus offers himself as a sacrifice back to God. This exchange of gifts restores the possibility of friendship between God and humanity. At the celebration of the Eucharist, when his flesh is shared as food, the restored friendship between God and humanity is fully realized. His command to his followers to eat his flesh and drink his blood is a command to come to the table of feasting at which God and humanity are joined.

But here we might get a little frustrated. Even know-ing that Jesus died as a sacrifice to take away the sins of the world, we still want to know why. Why didn't he just find another way to take away the sins of the world? Couldn't he have just declared, "I am the Son of God and I hereby take away the sins of the world"?

Well, yes. He does have the power to save humanity in any way he chooses. He could have saved humanity by standing on one foot.

But God is love; that is his nature. And saving humanity by standing on one foot is not fitting for one who loves perfectly. To save us in that way would not have allowed him to give everything he wanted to give to us. It would not have allowed him to show us how serious our sins are. It would not have allowed him to show us, in a graphic way, how much our salvation means to him, how much we mean to him.

God always acts in a way that is perfectly consistent with who he is: infinite love.

No human being—not even an angel, in fact—would choose what Jesus chooses to do, given the same power. In fact, Jesus points this out when the apostle Peter tries to convince him not to go to Jerusalem to die: "You are not on the side of God, but of men," Jesus tells him (Matt. 16:23).

God's way is not like our ways.

To understand what Jesus does on the cross, we must begin with an admission that God does not think as we do. He does not just want to save us; he wants to pay the price for our sins, and he wants to pay this price because he loves us perfectly and infinitely.

For us, if there is an easier way to get something done, we choose that. For God, because he is perfect love, such thinking will not do. Only the logic of perfect love will do. Only the logic that asks, "What is the most I can do for my beloved?" can be God's logic.

In suffering and dying on the cross, Jesus restores friendship between God and humanity in the most loving and respectful way possible. He fully respects human choices, even when humans reject him and torture him to death outside the walls of his own holy city.

His death outside Jerusalem is a perfect image of the depths of divine love. He comes in friendship as a teacher, healer, and exorcist. He offers himself, without reservation, as a servant of others. This is love in action. But he does not withdraw that love when he is rejected and insulted, abused, exiled from his own city, and killed as if he were of no value. This—the continuation of love even unto death—is consistent with his nature: love without limit.

He chose to save his beloved (you and me) in the manner that demanded everything of him because that is what divine love does. It is not love as humans love. Because we do not love as God loves, his sacrifice for us is hard, maybe even impossible, to comprehend. But it is very good news because it means we have nothing to fear from God, even when we have turned away from him in the most horrific and selfish ways. He has demonstrated this, and this demonstration is part of his love, too.

He wants us to see him as he is so that we will be comforted. He wants to be raised up high as he suffers so that all can see and, in seeing, know how close God is to them, how far he will go for them.

Before his crucifixion, he tells the apostles, "I, when I am lifted up from the earth, will draw all men to myself" (John 12:32). Seeing the depths of God's love demonstrated on the cross, no matter what we have done, we can join the apostle Paul in crying out:

> I am sure that neither death, nor life, nor angels, nor principalities, nor things present, nor things to come, nor powers, nor height, nor depth, nor anything else in all creation, will be able to separate us from the love of God in Christ Jesus our Lord" (Rom. 8:38–39).

PART TWO

WHAT JESUS TAUGHT

13

Jesus and Modern Values

John's Gospel begins,

In the beginning was the Word, and the Word was with
God, and the Word was God . . . And the Word became
flesh and dwelt among us, full of grace and truth; we have
beheld his glory, glory as of the only Son from the Father
. . . And from his fulness have we all received, grace upon
grace. For the law was given through Moses; grace and
truth came through Jesus Christ (John 1:1, 14, 16–17).

According to John, then, the first action in the life of Jesus
was that he, who was God, became a man. So far as John is
concerned, if you want to know what Jesus did, you start here.

The fact that his earliest followers thought that he was not
just born like any other person but came down from heav-
en is essential to what they presented him as doing when
they wrote about him. Even in being born, he was "doing"

things that no other person had done before or ever would do. And as he took up a public life, each thing he said and did had a special significance because each and every thing he said and did was a revelation of God.

When he went to a marriage feast, for example, just his presence taught something about how God sees such things such as marriages and feasts. Likewise, how he treated a woman caught in adultery revealed God's manner with women, with sexual sin, and with those who are cruel to women or who lack mercy toward sinners.

Thus, when his biographers tell us what Jesus did, they are always also telling us how it is with God, and, consequently, what our lives should be like if we desire to live as God intended.

We can sum up the biography of Jesus as understood by those who knew him like this: God loves us so much that he has become one of us. He has walked among us as a teacher, a healer, and an exorcist, giving us a perfect example of how to treat each other. He has called us and formed us into a new people. And, having done these things, he has given his life for us as a love offering, he has been laid in a tomb, he has been raised from the dead, and he has returned to heaven where he now reigns as king and where we will, if we remain in his friendship, join him one day.

In this section, as I try to give a basic account of his life and teaching, I will do so as one who accepts, as his earliest biographers did, that his is the story of the time God walked among us.

It seems to me that this is a fair way to present Jesus, even to the person who is not a believer, because it allows such a person the dignity of a straight answer about what Jesus did according to those who knew him—and to those who believe in him now.

With such a presentation, the reader can be informed enough to consider the strange story of the man Jesus, at least this once, and choose to accept it or reject it.

As soon as we begin to do this, however, we come face to face with an uncomfortable fact: The Jesus we meet in his biographies is not very modern. He teaches things, in fact, that sometimes differ quite sharply from "modern values." If we want the real Jesus, we will have to accept this about him.

There is no need to create an exaggerated enmity between Jesus and the modern world. His teachings are not anti-modern. There are many qualities of the modern world, in fact, that are carryovers from its Christian past, things that come from Jesus himself. But we must be sober in recognizing that Jesus does not always affirm modern values. And in some cases, he stands firmly against them.

In our day, this creates enough tension between "modern values" and "Christian values" that people who decide to take Jesus seriously can end up in an uncomfortable position: wanting Jesus, but finding that accepting him means giving up certain aspects of the current modern worldview.

There are many people, of course, who remain entirely enmeshed in modern ways of thinking about morals who also accept Jesus, but to do this, they must ignore or elide some of what Jesus says. Usually, this involves treating some of what Jesus said as merely reflecting his times and not reflecting what he would say if he were alive today.

Jesus, such people might reason, though a good man, did not have the benefit of modern progress. We have, they will say, progressed beyond some of the harsh things Jesus said about such things as sin or hell.

But here we are just trying to let Jesus speak for himself not merely as a man of the past, but as God become a man. This means listening to him not as a man merely embedded in history, but a person who, also, transcends history and teaches the truth for all time.

And, in any case, what if all moral "progress" isn't good? What if, sometimes, society goes backward morally? Nazism and Communism, the twin evil ideologies of the twentieth century, were hailed by their proponents as "progress," after all. The Nazis thought their beliefs were scientific, and the Communists thought all history inevitably moved in their direction. Both were wrong.

And what about our own moral situation? Would any of us really argue that the consumerist and even hedonistic culture that emerged in the 1950s and 60s and has now spread throughout the free world is really an advance for humanity?

Indeed, the harshness and selfishness of the modern world, the disfiguring of nature, and the isolation that modern people feel from one another all prompt us to ask, "Is this really progress?"

I am convinced that, in our hearts, most of us sense that the modern world is not progressing in love and kindness and happiness—the very things that Jesus taught. That, instead, we are losing important human dimensions, we are becoming strangers to one another, and we feel increasingly empty and cold.

My friend, the teachings of Jesus can be difficult, but they are not cold. They are filled with the warmth of friendship and feasting. In fact, that is exactly what Jesus offers: friendship and a feast. If he is, as the apostle Paul claims, "the image of the invisible God," then, in him, we see God revealed as a healer and a friend, a person who cooks breakfast for his companions but is not afraid to physically confront those who would cheat the poor or keep them from approaching God in his temple.

This is a person with the fire of real love, and a great passion for justice, within him.

He calls out to the whole world "Come to me," and he shares everything he has with anyone who accepts his invitation.

I mention the inner dissonance that a fully modern person sometimes experiences when confronting the moral teaching of Jesus only because an awareness of this dissonance might make it easier to consider, at least this once, what he has to say.

He was a person who was very comfortable with making others uncomfortable, but he does not do so gratuitously. Even when he speaks harshly, he does so to draw us into a life of love.

But oddly, it is "love" that most brings Jesus into conflict with "modern values" because love, as Jesus teaches it, is at odds with modern ideas about love.

Because Jesus stands against many modern ideas about what constitutes love, many modern people hesitate to turn to Jesus as the Lord of Love. To them, to accept Jesus means giving up a worldview they aren't ready to give up.

No matter how much they might ache for the kind of intimate friendship with God that Jesus offers, and no matter how much they might even desire to participate in the hardships of self-giving that Jesus calls his followers to, they will not surrender to him because they see such surrender as a surrender of progress.

I believe they are wrong in this. I know that if they would surrender to Jesus they would not find themselves slipping back into a darker time, but would find themselves loved and able to love, accepted and able to accept, at peace and generous in offering peace to others.

But what argument is powerful enough to entice another person to let go of an entire worldview? I know I do not have such an argument. Nor do I think that arguments, alone, can convince anyone to accept the view of the world that Jesus presents. Only meeting him will do that, and it is up to each person to decide whether or not to seek such a meeting.

With that in mind, I will try to let the teachings and actions of Jesus speak for themselves as we grapple with the question of this section of the book, "What did Jesus do?"

In this section, of his three primary actions—teaching, healing, and casting out demons—I will focus overwhelmingly on Jesus' teaching.

I do this not to dismiss or deny his miracles, but because I think that his teachings, in fact, pose the greater difficulty for those of us alive today, in the latter part of the modern era. It is my view that modern people would, for the most part, have little trouble accepting the miracles of Jesus if they did not find his teaching so hard to harmonize with what the modern world proposes about morals.

Let's begin, then, at the very point where the life and call of Jesus pose the greatest difficulty in our day, with his teaching about the moral life.

Jesus and Sex

Jesus taught chastity as a moral requirement. This put him in sync with traditional Jewish teaching and with the teachings of many pagan schools of thought. But in some ways it put him out of sync with what was accepted in the ancient world.

Just to give a harsh example, what we think of today as rape was not even thought of as a crime in many ancient settings. Many of the people in the Roman Empire were slaves and could be raped without recourse by those who owned them. Wives could be raped by husbands. Soldiers often raped with impunity.

Nowhere in the ancient world were women thought of as the equals of men, and it was common for a woman who had been sexually assaulted, for example, to be treated not as a victim but as the one who had acted criminally.

Jesus lived as a virgin and treated women with a radically new kind of respect. In a world where a divorced woman became extremely vulnerable to exploitation, he taught that a man could not divorce his wife. In a world where women were not permitted to engage in public discourse, he conversed openly with women, taught them as students, and, on several occasions, used his moral authority to protect women who were persecuted.

It is hard for us—we who live in a world of human rights and the expectation of equal treatment for men and women—to grasp just how radically new the complete sexual ethic of Jesus was. In a world of tolerated sexual violence and exploitation, he taught an ethic of self-restraint, respect, and equality. He even treated children with respect and welcome.

These teachings about the equality of the sexes, the value of children, and the need for restraint so that all could be respected were, over the next few centuries after his death, to utterly transform the Roman world and then go on to transform most of the rest of the world.

As the world now rebels against Christian sexual ethics and mocks this transformation, they betray a short memory of how it ennobled and protected billions of human lives, in ways that the world takes for granted.

14

An Exchange of Gifts

When Jesus first sends his apostles on a mission of their own, he tells them, "Preach as you go, saying, 'The kingdom of heaven is at hand.' Heal the sick, raise the dead, cleanse lepers, cast out demons. You received without pay, give without pay" (Matt. 10:7–8).

The moral life that Jesus teaches here and throughout the Gospels can be summed up this way: join Jesus in his mission by freely giving to others what you have received. It is a morality of imitation in that Jesus' disciples are to say what he says and do what he does (for example, proclaim the kingdom of God, heal the sick, etc.), and it is a morality of cooperation in that they are to extend his work far and wide.

The morality that Jesus teaches is not a moral program that can be separated from himself. He came preaching the kingdom of God, healing others, and casting out demons. He fed the poor and encouraged the oppressed. Indeed, these are things he did for his own followers—for example, casting demons out of Mary Magdalene (Mark 16:9)—and now they must do these things for others.

We modern people tend to be individualists, and we expect morality to be about things that an individual should and shouldn't do. But Jesus does not teach mere individualist morality—a list of morally excellent things for you to do on your own as best you can. Rather, he sends his friends, his brothers and sisters, into the world to work together and to extend to others the gifts they received from him.

Early Christians called this new gift-centered manner of living "the way," and they understood its moral and religious dimensions to be simply two sides of a single reality. The religious practices he teaches are meant to confer divine gifts that make it possible for his followers to give as he gave, even to the point of self-sacrifice.

Because the spiritual gifts he gives are a prerequisite to the moral life he teaches—a life of imitating him and sharing him with others—Jesus insisted, sometimes vehemently, that we should never try to live the morality he teaches on our own. To live the fullness of the moral life as Jesus teaches it, we must remain, at all times, connected to him:

> I am the true vine, and my Father is the vinedresser. Every branch of mine that bears no fruit, he takes away, and every branch that does bear fruit he prunes, that it may bear more fruit. You are already made clean by the word which I have spoken to you. Abide in me, and I in you. As the branch cannot bear fruit by itself, unless it abides

in the vine, neither can you, unless you abide in me. I am the vine, you are the branches. He who abides in me, and I in him, he it is that bears much fruit, for apart from me you can do nothing (John 15:1–5).

Being called to receive gifts and being sent to share gifts. Being detached from the world in order to be firmly attached to Jesus. These are the core elements of the strange and challenging life that he teaches. We can't follow him without putting him at the center of all things. We can't abstract his moral teaching out into some theory or sum it up in axioms because morality is about gift—and the gift given and received is himself.

At one point, he describes how he will judge all the nations at the end of time. He will reward and punish people based on how they treated him, personally. To those he welcomes into his kingdom he will say:

"For I was hungry and you gave me food, I was thirsty and you gave me drink, I was a stranger and you welcomed me, I was naked and you clothed me, I was sick and you visited me, I was in prison and you came to me." Then the righteous will answer him, "Lord, when did we see thee hungry and feed thee, or thirsty and give thee drink? And when did we see thee a stranger and welcome thee, or naked and clothe thee? And when did we see thee sick or in prison and visit thee?" And the King will answer them, "Truly, I say to you, as you did it to one of the least of these my brethren, you did it to me" (Matt. 25:35–40).

In a similar way, he makes himself central to human moral calculations when, in John's Gospel, he gives what he calls "a new command." He tells his followers, "Even as I have loved you . . . also love one another" (John 13:34).

This command is not only new in the sense that it hadn't been given before; in fact it could not possibly have been given before. For it is not a general law, like the commandments against murder or stealing; it is a specific presentation of himself as the ultimate measure of morality.

The fullness of the moral law is not a theory or a system, but a person: Jesus. The moral life, in its fullness, consists in loving him and imitating him by giving ourselves to others—the sick, the imprisoned, the hungry, and so on—as he did. To paraphrase St. Francis de Sales, the measure of the truly good life is that it loves without measure, as Jesus did.

In this sense, the moral teaching of Jesus is radical. It presents an example for moral living—his own life of total self-giving—as the standard for everyone in all times and in all places.

One more thing must be said about the unique moral life into which Jesus calls his followers: because it is a morality of imitation in which we are to give as Jesus gives, it requires total self-giving. In fact, the image that Jesus uses to explain the morality into which he is calling his friends is his own cross:

Then Jesus told his disciples, "If any man would come after me, let him deny himself and take up his cross and follow me. For whoever would save his life will lose it, and whoever loses his life for my sake will find it. For what will it profit a man, if he gains the whole world and forfeits his life? Or what shall a man give in return for his life? For the Son of man is to come with his angels in the glory of his Father, and then he will repay every man for what he has done" (Matt. 16:24–27).

There is consolation at the end of this teaching. Jesus will come again in glory and reward those who imitate him, which means that he's not just teaching a philosophy of endless self-negation. No, the life that Jesus calls his followers into involves a heavenly dimension that is hidden now, but that gives the whole thing its final meaning. It all ends in heavenly glory.

Still, there is no denying the cross.

The way of life, so to speak, passes through death. This is a radical call to live for others, as Jesus did, even when to do so costs everything.

Jesus and Money

Jesus had wealthy financial supporters, he had a treasurer for his little community, he taught people to pay their taxes, and he never condemned property or money as such.

He also called at least some of his followers to join him in a life of personal poverty. He did not seem to have owned much of anything himself, and he regularly said things such as, "Blessed are the poor." He even went so far as to say, "Woe to you who are rich, for you have received your consolation," and "woe to you who are filled now, for you will be hungry" (Luke 6:24–25).

So how do we make sense of his teachings on money? Like everything else he said and did, it's best understood in the context of his invitation to repent and participate in the kingdom of God. Jesus calls each person to turn from a worldly life and toward the coming kingdom. Where money serves the kingdom of God, or at least does not interfere with it, he seems to see it as a tool like any tool. But where it puts us in conflict with the kingdom, it is dangerous in the extreme.

Participation in the kingdom of God means being "consoled" and being "filled" in ways that money and food cannot do. The members of God's kingdom are all consoled and fed by God directly, and, in turn, they console one another and feed one another.

The rich, those who are filled with the things of this world, are in grave danger because it is harder for them to detach from the world to attach to God, and they are in danger because love of their own wealth can make them cold to the needs of others. Thus, wealth tempts one away from following the two great commandments—love of God and love of neighbor.

Like everyone else who succumbs to temptation, those whose riches tempt them away from love of God and love of neighbor must repent of their selfishness if they are to share in the kingdom of God. They must become detached from money and return to humble dependence on God. What is more, they must rekindle love of neighbor within themselves and cheerfully share what they have with the poor.

Money, if they do these things, is not an obstacle to their entering the kingdom of God but a doorway to it because, as St. Paul said, "God loves a cheerful giver" (2 Cor. 9:7). Freed from the allure of money and restored to love of God and neighbor, they will be able to enter the sharing of gifts that constitutes God's kingdom.

15

Moral Minimums vs. the Way of Perfection

Even as we affirm that the moral teaching of Jesus is radically new—a morality of self-giving love modeled on Jesus, himself—we have to admit that most of the moral teaching of Jesus is not very innovative.

In most cases, when he is asked moral questions, he replies in ways that are entirely familiar to his Jewish listeners:

And behold, one came up to him, saying, "Teacher, what good deed must I do, to have eternal life?" And he said to him, "Why do you ask me about what is good? One there is who is good. If you would enter life, keep the commandments." He said to him, "Which?" And Jesus said, "You shall not kill, You shall not commit adultery, You shall not steal, You shall not bear false witness, Honor your father and mother, and, You shall love your neighbor as yourself" (Matt. 19:16–19).

Here Jesus adds nothing to the traditional Jewish understanding of morality as summed up in the commandments. What he tells the young man is exactly what Moses would have said 1,200 years earlier.

The young man will follow up with another question and Jesus will give a different kind of answer. But here Jesus gives a normal Jewish answer to the question of what "must" be done to receive eternal life. "Must" implies the minimum, and Jesus gives the minimum: "Keep the commandments." He gives a similar answer to similar questions in other Gospels.

If you want moral minimums, he makes it clear, they are available without reference to himself. Human beings have a natural moral sense. We can reason about what is right and wrong, and we can intuit that we are meant to do what is right and avoid what is wrong.

To this natural grasp of morality, Jewish teaching adds the deeper moral insights gained from the Jewish relationship with God, beginning with the two great commandments: "You shall love the LORD your God with all your heart, and with all your soul, and with all your might" (Deut. 6:5), and "You shall love your neighbor as yourself" (Lev. 19:18).

Jesus does not reject either the natural sense of morality or the moral teachings revealed in the Old Testament. But he surpasses them both, finally revealing the entirety of the moral law. It is greater than natural intuition and greater than any list of commandments. It is not a theory or a system, but a person: Jesus.

Back to the young man who asked what good he must do to gain eternal life. He is not satisfied when Jesus tells him to keep the commandments. This young man knows there is more to what Jesus is teaching, so he tries to get Jesus to tell him the something more:

> The young man said to him, "All these I have observed; what do I still lack?" Jesus said to him, "If you would be perfect, go, sell what you possess and give to the poor, and you will have treasure in heaven; and come, follow me" (Matt. 19:20–21).

With these words, Jesus seems to answer the question "What do I still lack?" in two ways. He seems to be telling the young man that he lacks perfect charity toward the poor. But he also seems to be telling the young man that what he lacks is Jesus, himself.

If the young man will be charitable and follow Jesus, he will have what he lacks.

This is perfection—to lack neither charity nor the company of Jesus.

To "follow" Jesus has two meanings here. One is to "follow" his example and the other is to go where he goes. In following the example of the detachment and charity of Jesus, the young man can become free to accompany him, to be in his company and the company of his friends, to share fully in their charitable way of life and become one of them.

Like the young man, the "scholar of the law" who asks a similar question in Luke's chapter ten presses Jesus to go beyond his first answer. Unlike the young man, who is sincerely seeking answers, the scholar of the law, we are told, is testing Jesus. (Probably for this reason, he does not get the same invitation to follow that the young man gets.)

When Jesus affirms the standard rabbinical answer to his question—that love of God and love of neighbor are the keys to eternal life—the scholar presses on, asking, "And who is my neighbor?" Jesus replies with a parable:

"A man was going down from Jerusalem to Jericho, and he fell among robbers, who stripped him and beat him, and departed, leaving him half dead. Now by chance a priest was going down that road; and when he saw him he passed by on the other side. So likewise a Levite, when he came to the place and saw him, passed by on the other side. But a Samaritan, as he journeyed, came to where he was; and when he saw him, he had compassion, and went to him and bound up his wounds, pouring on oil and wine; then he set him on his own beast and brought him to an inn, and took care of him. And the next day he took out two denarii and gave them to the innkeeper, saying, 'Take care of him; and whatever more you spend, I will repay you when I come back.' Which of these three, do you think, proved neighbor to the man who fell among the robbers?" He said, "The one who showed mercy on him." And Jesus said to him, "Go and do likewise" (Luke 10:30–37).

Here, Jesus is giving the word neighbor its widest possible meaning. He chooses the Samaritan as the hero of the story precisely because Samaritans and Jews were neighbors . . . who despised one another. Likely, the scholar of the law also despised the Samaritans, which makes this story a bit of a tweak at him. But Jesus does reveal to him the most perfect way to interpret the moral law.

Jesus' answer to the rich young man, however, is the only one that can truly open the moral law—the law of love—in a permanent sense: "Come, follow me" (Matt. 19:21).

It is only by following and imitating Jesus that we can learn all he wants us to learn. But, sadly, the rich young man did not follow. Instead, he "went away sorrowful; for he had great possessions" (Matt. 19:22). Had he accepted the invitation, he would have ended up where the apostles ended up—in Jerusalem with Jesus as he went to his death. He would have suffered, but his suffering would not have been the whole story.

What Jesus offered the young man was "perfection," and the fear of suffering loss and hardship kept the young man from receiving it. He settled, rather, for a comfortable life.

This is one of those places where what Jesus teaches seems to conflict at a root level with what modern people believe. A mature person in our day is supposed to accept that moral

perfection is impossible. In inviting the young man to follow him, Jesus suggests otherwise. When Jesus says, "if you
wish to become perfect," he implies that perfection is exactly what will come to those who follow.

Jesus and True Peace

In Matthew's Gospel, Jesus says these strange words:

> "Do not think that I have come to bring peace on earth;
> I have not come to bring peace, but a sword. For I have
> come to set a man against his father, and a daughter
> against her mother, and a daughter-in-law against her
> mother-in-law; and a man's foes will be those of his own
> household" (Matt. 10:34–35).

Why would Jesus say this when he speaks constantly of
peace and is constantly blessing people with peace? Isn't he
the one who said, "Blessed are the peacemakers, for they shall
be called sons of God?" (Matt. 5:9).

How can we reconcile these things?

We get a hint of how to reconcile them in John's Gospel when
Jesus says, "Peace I leave with you; my peace I give to you; not
as the world gives do I give to you" (John 14:27). The peace that
Jesus gives is not like the "peace" that the world gives.

Consider the Pax Romana—the great Roman age of peace
in which he lived. It was a false peace insofar as keeping it required horrific brutality and constant injustice. Clearly, this is
not the kind of peace Jesus wants for his people. He has come
to bring a peace rooted in truth and love; but this new ethic
will cause friction with those who promote the Roman kind of

peace. Thus, he has come to bring "the sword," in the sense that great division will erupt as a consequence of his teaching.

To understand the kind of peace he does want, we must turn to the Hebrew scriptures, which are, in a certain sense, a thousand-year exploration of the source of true peace. For example, 700 years before Jesus, speaking of the consequences of unfaithfulness to God, the prophet Micah wrote, "For the son belittles his father, the daughter rises up against her mother, the daughter-in-law against her mother-in-law, and your enemies are members of your household. But as for me, I will look to the LORD, I will wait for God my savior" (Mic. 7:6–7).

Clearly, in the words recorded in Matthew that we read above, Jesus is referring to this passage. He wants us to refer to Micah when we consider his own words about peace. And, indeed, Micah gives us a magnificent clue about the source of true peace when he says, "I will wait for God my savior."

These words, "God my savior," are almost a perfect translation of the name Jesus. He himself is true peace.

16

Morality, the Trinity, and the Interior Life

"You, therefore, must be perfect, as your heavenly Father is perfect" (Matt. 5:48).

This teaching of Jesus would not go over well at a modern school, where we teach children that they don't have to be perfect because we love them as they are. Before we finish with our little review of Jesus' moral teaching, we are going to have to grapple with this difficult sentence. What does he mean by it? Do we really have to be perfect?

Answering that question will not only allow us to sharpen our understanding of what Jesus taught about morality—it will give us an insight into his teaching about the nature of God.

All Christians profess a belief in the Trinity: that God is three persons who each possess the single divine nature. The word doesn't appear in the New Testament, but later Christians came to use it as shorthand for what Jesus revealed to his apostles about God.

For example, at the end of Matthew's Gospel, Jesus gives a command that has since come to be called the Great Commission: "Go therefore and make disciples of all nations, baptizing them in the name of the Father and of the Son and of the Holy Spirit" (Matt. 28:19).

When this instruction is taken in the context of Jesus' other teachings, it is clear that Jesus understands the Father, Son, and Holy Spirit to be distinct divine persons. Each is God. However, Jesus never abandons the Jewish teaching that God is one. Rather, he holds two positions that, on the surface, seem contradictory: one God, three persons.

This revelation of God's nature is new with Jesus, but we do not see him teaching the doctrine like a theology professor. Rather, we see him living as a divine person in communion with the Father and Holy Spirit, both of whom are treated as every bit as divine as himself. Above all, Jesus reveals that the one God is three persons by his manner of living and praying.

One powerful instance of this happens in Luke's Gospel after Jesus reaches an important milestone in the founding of his Church. He sends out seventy-two of those who are closest to him on a mission to prepare other people to receive him. This is the first time he calls this whole group to go out as a Church into the world: "Whenever you enter a town and they receive you, eat what is set before you; heal the sick in it and say to them, 'The kingdom of God has come near to you'" (Luke 10:8–9).

When his new church returns from its mission, Jesus is elated, and he even tells them that he has seen Satan fall. And then:

> In that same hour he rejoiced in the Holy Spirit and said, "I thank thee, Father, Lord of heaven and earth, that thou hast hidden these things from the wise and understanding and revealed them to babes; yea, Father, for such was thy gracious will. All things have been delivered to me by my Father; and no one knows who the Son is except the Father, or who the Father is except the Son and any one to whom the Son chooses to reveal him" (Luke 10:21–22).

This especially elated moment of prayer is presented to his assembled Church as a trinitarian moment. They gather around him who they know as Messiah and Lord; they see him rejoice in the Holy Spirit; they hear him praise the Father and speak of how he and the Father know each other. Then, in the next chapter of the same Gospel, Jesus tells the people that their "heavenly Father" will "give the Holy Spirit to those who ask him" (Luke 11:13).

This teaching of one God, three persons is not a theological abstraction for scholars but part of the good news for all of us. If God is not a single, monolithic personage but is three persons in love, we can participate in the inner life of God. Here God is the family, and because Jesus became one of us, we can be adopted into that family as his brothers and sisters. By being made brothers and sisters of Jesus, we are made sons and daughters of the Father. And if we are sons and daughters, we are participants in the household of God. We have become drawn into the inner life of the divine.

Now, this is just an analogy, and like all analogies that try to explain God's nature, it's necessarily imperfect. God is not a family, for instance, in the same respects that a human family is. But by this analogy, we can begin to grasp how the teaching of Jesus opens a new possibility for us. If what Jesus is teaching is true, then we can participate in the inner life of God. It's a world-changer.

For this reason, we must take with grave seriousness Jesus' command that we are to be perfect as our Father in heaven is perfect. For this moral teaching is connected to our final destiny, which is to share in the divine life. And we can't do that while at the same time holding onto sin and evil because those things are negations of God and refusals of his friendship.

God is love. What happens in the inner life of God is pure love. We cannot enter there unless we are made capable of pure love ourselves, which can't happen as long as we cling to imperfections or refuse the help of God in overcoming them. Jesus' moral teaching, then, is not meant just to make us better, nicer people. It's meant to make us God's adopted sons and daughters, to prepare us for union with the Trinity.

I would like to turn to a section in the Sermon on the Mount for a moment. As you read it, think about those familiar words now in that new context. Consider that what Jesus is teaching is not just a list of his moral demands but a way of life meant to prepare each of us for perfect divine intimacy.

As Jesus begins this moral instruction (one that many people have called the greatest moral teaching in the history of the world) he makes clear that his purpose is to help those who are listening to "enter into the kingdom of heaven." When he gets to his hardest moral instruction, he tells them that they should love their enemies, "that you may be children of your heavenly Father."

He concludes it with the words we have already discussed, "be perfect, just as your heavenly Father is perfect." He wants them (and us) to enter the kingdom of heaven and be made children of God, which means achieving moral and spiritual perfection.

Jesus and the Forgiveness of Sins

Jesus went about preaching as a prophet of repentance and an extravagant forgiver of sin. On the night before he died, Jesus said that the pouring out of his blood was for "the forgiveness of sins." But why is Jesus so concerned with sin? Why does he go about forgiving sins, even handing on to his Church the power to do it? It can be very hard for a modern person to understand what this means.

Sin is not a scientific category. We cannot measure it with instruments or treat it with medicines, and we tend to think only things that can be measured and treated in this way are real. If something is wrong, we seek a therapy for it—whether that therapy is medical or social or psychological.

But sin is not that kind of problem. To sin, in the biblical sense, is to act unjustly. It is to fail to give to another what is due. Because we are social creatures, and cannot exist or find happiness on our own, such behavior damages a person at the very root. It damages our ability to share life with others—most especially with God—and for creatures who need others, this is a kind of death.

What we owe to other people depends on our relationship to them, their needs, our needs, and various other factors. At the very least, we owe other people their basic human rights, but for some people, like our parents, we owe much more than the minimum.

What we owe to God, on the other hand, is absolute: we owe God everything because everything we have is a gift from him and because he is the rightful master of all creation. What is more, God is perfectly good, just, merciful, and loving, and it is wrong to mistreat one who always treats us with goodness, justice, mercy, and love. The most common way we sin against God is to set our hearts on things that are less than God while we refuse to give our hearts to God, the giver of life who is all good and deserving of all our love.

There is no therapy or medical intervention that will fix things when we have failed to give God or our fellow humans what is due to them. Sin, understood this way, is not a problem merely of the self, but of relationship to others.

The cure for sin is to repair relationships. The one who has done harm must repent, and the one harmed must forgive. Because Jesus is God made man, he can forgive every sin. He can offer divine forgiveness, and he wants to do it. He does so continually throughout his public life, even instructing his followers, as we said, to go on forgiving sin in his name after his death.

This forgiveness is key to his overall mission, which is to restore friendship between God and humanity: "For God did not send his Son into the world to condemn the world, but that the world might be saved through him" (John 3:17).

17

Religion as Preparation for Life with God

Jesus' moral teaching—which demands perfection—seems impossible. How can any person avoid not just murder and adultery but, also, give up any interior disposition toward rage or lust, greed or pride?

But Jesus insists that his teaching is not only possible, but easy!

> Come to me, all who labor and are heavy laden, and I will give you rest. Take my yoke upon you, and learn from me; for I am gentle and lowly in heart, and you will find rest for your souls. For my yoke is easy, and my burden is light (Matt. 11:28–30).

The burden he lays on us is perfection, and then he tells us that his burden is light. How can we reconcile these things?

The short answer is that Jesus intends to do the work for us. Consider this story (actually, just the first part of an extended story) from John's Gospel:

As he passed by, he saw a man blind from his birth. And his disciples asked him, "Rabbi, who sinned, this man or his parents, that he was born blind?" Jesus answered, "It was not that this man sinned, or his parents, but that the works of God might be made manifest in him. We must work the works of him who sent me, while it is day; night comes, when no one can work. As long as I am in the world, I am the light of the world." As he said this, he spat on the ground and made clay of the spittle and anointed the man's eyes with the clay, saying to him, "Go, wash in the pool of Siloam" (which means Sent). So he went and washed and came back seeing" (John 9:1–7).

Here, Jesus does a lot in a short space: he rebukes any superstitious understanding of physical disability, he makes a prophecy of his own death, and he refers to himself as the light of the world. And then Jesus heals the man, but in a very odd way.

Before we discuss how Jesus heals this man, remember that in John's Gospel Jesus can heal and even raise people from the dead merely with a word. Just a few chapters earlier he healed a man who had been unable to walk for thirty-eight years merely by saying, "Rise, take up your pallet, and walk" (John 5:8). Understanding this, we can understand that Jesus is not just healing the blind man in this passage, but is doing so in a way that conveys layers of meaning. We are supposed to ask, "Why did he do it that way?" And when we do, we get a powerful teaching about Jesus, himself.

Many commentaries on this story will point out that Jesus heals with the dirt of the earth, which is exactly what God used in the book of Genesis to create Adam. Jesus is not just healing the man; he is doing so in a way that re-enacts the first creation of humanity by God.

This re-enactment of creation is two things: a sign that Jesus is God (he acts as God acts) and a sign that "the work of the one who sent" him is a work of re-creation. The work of Jesus is to remake humanity.

This is also why the Gospel writer emphasizes that the healed man was born blind and did not become blind later. To have been born blind is, in a sense, to have been blind from one's very creation. To heal such blindness is not just to fix an injury but to remake the person, as if from the beginning. Later in this story, the idea of re-creation is further emphasized in an almost comic scene when the blind man's friends are no longer sure he is the same man. "The neighbors and those who had seen him before as a beggar, said, 'Is not this the man who used to sit and beg?' Some said, 'It is he'; others said, 'No, but he is like him.' He said, 'I am the man'" (John 9:8–9).

Once we see that the mission of Jesus is not just to provide a new teaching but to re-create us, we can begin to see how Jesus, who lays on his followers the burden of being perfect as the Father in heaven is, can also say that his burden is light.

Jesus intends to remake you and me. The work of perfecting is his, not ours. It is he who will make us perfect. Healing the blind is a sign that he can do it.

But here we must make a strange observation: the actions of Jesus do not immediately heal the blind man. You might be tempted to assume that Jesus healed him by smearing clay on his eyes, but that is not what happened. Rather, the story says that Jesus told him, "Go wash in the Pool of Siloam." So he went and washed, and then came back able to see.

In other words, Jesus sent him off to perform a kind of ritual—washing in a special pool—and it was in the man's performance of this ritual washing that Jesus (who started the work by making the clay and applying it to the man's eyes) finishes the work of "re-creating" the man. This ritual washing puts us in mind of baptism, the ritual that Jesus' Church would soon use, at his command, to remake people spiritually, causing them to be born again of water and the Spirit.

The interior perfection to which Jesus calls his followers is similar to the sight of the blind man in this story. Nothing the blind man can do on his own can recover his sight. Nothing we can do can make us perfect as our Father in heaven is perfect. Only Jesus has the power to do these things, and he does them on his own initiative—in this case, without the blind man even asking.

But note he does not heal the man without the man's cooperation. The blind man could have refused or failed to do what Jesus asked, and he would, it seems, not have been healed. What is more—and this is vital to understanding

Jesus' religious teaching—Jesus connects his healing power to a physical action. What he accomplishes far exceeds what this physical action normally would cause, of course, but he does actually accomplish it through this physical act. Washing, on its own, does not repair a damaged physical organ; but washing when Jesus has commanded heals miraculously.

If Jesus fills an act with power, then it has power. Here, in miniature, we have the entire religion that Jesus teaches:

- On his own initiative he comes with saving power, offering to remake people.

- He leaves it up to the other person whether he wants to participate in this remaking or not.

- He accomplishes this remaking through physical acts commanded by himself and filled with his power.

- When his commands are followed, and these physical acts are performed, people receive what he has promised.

We also see Jesus commanding physical actions and conferring on them his own divine power at the Last Supper. On the night before he died, after eating the Passover meal with the apostles, he

took bread, and when he had given thanks, he broke it, and said, "This is my body which is for you. Do this in remembrance of me." In the same way also the cup, after supper, saying, "This cup is the new covenant in my blood. Do this, as often as you drink it, in remembrance of me" (1 Cor. 11:24–25).

This event is recounted in the Gospels, but I have chosen here to give the text of this event as written by Paul in his letter to the Corinthians, for two reasons. First, Paul's letters, though they are the earliest Christian writings, do not include many direct quotes from Jesus. They are letters, after all, not biographies. The fact that Paul chooses to relate these particular words so precisely shows their importance to the very earliest Christians.

Second, there is almost universal agreement among scholars that Paul is using a formula that his audience was familiar with, constituting a communal prayer in broad use by Christians at the time Paul wrote this letter (about two decades after the death of Jesus). This means that the very earliest Christians were doing just what Jesus had commanded them to do. They were repeating the physical acts of Jesus "in remembrance" of him.

From the context in Paul's letter, we know that they were gathering to do this each Sunday. A leader of the community was taking bread, blessing it and breaking it to share with others while saying the very words Jesus said, "This is my body, that is for you." And then this leader was doing likewise with the wine while saying, "This cup is the new covenant in my blood."

The religion that Jesus' earliest followers practiced was centered on these physical acts that Jesus had commanded—

especially baptism and the Sunday Eucharist, but also others such as anointing the sick and laying hands on those who are to receive the Holy Spirit—because they believed that Jesus had filled these acts with supernatural power.

About a century later, the Christian writer Justin Martyr gave the emperor Antoninus Pius a detailed description of what early Christians thought and did:

We do not consume the eucharistic bread and wine as if it were ordinary food and drink, for we have been taught that as Jesus Christ our Savior became a man of flesh and blood by the power of the Word of God, so also the food that our flesh and blood assimilates for its nourishment becomes the flesh and blood of the incarnate Jesus by the power of his own words contained in the prayer of thanksgiving.

The apostles, in their recollections, which are called Gospels, handed down to us what Jesus commanded them to do. They tell us that he took bread, gave thanks and said: Do this in memory of me. This is my body. In the same way he took the cup, he gave thanks and said: This is my blood. The Lord gave this command to them alone. Ever since then we have constantly reminded one another of these things. The rich among us help the poor and we are always united. For all that we receive we praise the creator of the universe through his Son Jesus Christ and through the Holy Spirit.[3]

3   First Apology

Today, Christians around the world still practice the same religion that Justin here describes for the emperor. Exactly the same.

Jesus does not explain why he chose to create a religion in which physical signs convey supernatural power, but one reason that makes sense is access. He who reigns from heaven but has not yet returned to take up his final reign on Earth did not want to leave his people without access to him and his power as they awaited his return. Each of the seven sacraments that he established is meant to give people this access to Jesus, in ways that combine matter and spirit just as we are combinations of matter and spirit.

With this in mind, we can return to the problem of being perfect as our Father in heaven is perfect.

Just as sight came to the blind man without him having to do anything of great difficulty, so does the power to reach moral and spiritual perfection come to those who receive the sacraments. The blind man's burden was easy—just go to the Pool of Siloam and wash. In the same way, in the religion of Jesus, our burdens are easy—just get baptized, receive the Eucharist, accept the words of forgiveness, and so on. These very small actions done in obedience to Jesus bring about our total remaking at his hands.

If he can make us out of clay, if he can heal with a little clay and a little washing, he can restore our souls through sacraments so long as we, like the blind man, trust him and do our little part.

Jesus and Eternal Life

Jesus said, "I came that they may have life, and have it abundantly" (John 10:10).

What is the abundance of life that Jesus offers? He seems to answer this question definitively a few chapters later when he says, "I am the way, and the truth, and the life" (John 14:6).

He, as God, is the source of life, and to have life in all its abundance is to possess him as a friend. Jesus calls his disciples into friendship to make them possessors of God.

But he does not say it is easy to possess God. He is not the salesman of an easy life.

He said:

If any man would come after me, let him deny himself and take up his cross and follow me. For whoever would save his life will lose it; and whoever loses his life for my sake and the gospel's will save it. For what does it profit a man, to gain the whole world and forfeit his life? For what can a man give in return for his life? (Mark 8:34–37).

The world has rejected God, and we as individuals have often rejected God, and so we must turn from the world and die to ourselves if we are to return to God.

As radical as this sounds, this is not really a radical message. Most religions, most self-help programs, most philosophies grasp that change is hard. Body builders even coined the phrase, "No pain, no gain."

But what is radical is that Jesus is not just teaching a philosophy of sacrifice for a greater good; he names the good he is offering as "the fullness of life," or even "eternal life." He is saying that those who imitate him ("take up your cross") will receive everything forever.

Many modern people dismiss this as a fairy-tale promise. But it is not. It is Jesus speaking plainly about hard-headed reality. He acknowledges that humanity has rejected God, but he does not condemn people for this but invites them back into friendship with him. As part of that invitation, he reveals a hidden truth about God, that God, though one being, is three persons.

This revelation makes clear that the fullness of life—the life that is God—is shared. The eternal God is not a remote, lonely figure, but three persons who share life perfectly. To be the creatures made in the image of this God means that we, too, are made to be shared, to share life, even to share in the life of God.

This is the invitation Jesus makes: to participate in the sharing of life and love that God intended from the beginning. Not to be cut off from him but to be with him; not to be cut off from one another but to be together as a people who love one another.

Our death to our own self-centeredness is required not because God wants us to perform tasks and get rewards, but because he is giving himself to us, and if we are not the kind of people who can surrender and give ourselves as he gives himself, we cannot join in the great eternal life of giving and sharing that is the life of the triune God.

18

Religion as Life with God

The sacramental religion that Jesus taught may sound too easy to be true. Does he really teach that, like the blind man at the Pool of Siloam, any person can be re-created? Does he really teach that he will do this for us without cost?

Many well-meaning people will rush in with all kinds of reminders about how we have to "take up our cross each day" and do other hard things if we really want to have what Jesus offers, but we should not be too quick to do so. De-emphasizing the power of Jesus' sacraments in favor of the difficult things we have to do gives a distorted picture of Christianity—turning it into a religion based on feats of physical suffering and spiritual athletics.

Above all, the religion Jesus taught is a religion of gratuitous healing and restoration. He was, and remains, a person of gratuitous healing and restoration. Nothing about Jesus is clearer than this.

Consider, for example, how Matthew describes his manner among people:

> Jesus went about all the cities and villages, teaching in their synagogues and preaching the gospel of the kingdom, and healing every disease and every infirmity. When he saw the crowds, he had compassion for them, because they were harassed and helpless, like sheep without a shepherd (Matt. 9:35–36).

By teaching, healing, and shepherding with compassion he shows his great desire to restore and care for others. How could the religion he founded be otherwise? If those who follow him are to be connected to him like branches on a vine then they are to be like him and their religion is to be an extension of him who gave away his healing and love without cost.

He is unconstrained in dispensing his gifts, freely and miraculously healing "every disease and every infirmity."

Sometimes Christians who believe that the generosity of Jesus means that his sacraments instantly and without cost remake those who have done even the most terrible things—so long as they will repent and accept the sacraments—are asked a hard question: "What if a man were to live his entire life doing evil to others and living for his own pleasure. And then, as the man was dying, a priest came into his room and told him the good news. If the man believed and was baptized just the moment before he died, would that one act really remake him and save him?"

If we accept that baptism, like all the sacraments, is what Jesus taught it to be—an action filled with his own divine power—then the answer is yes. An utterly corrupt and evil life can be made holy and pure instantaneously and for free.

This is what Christians mean by being "saved." By divine power, what was lost is restored, what was dead is made alive, what had become corrupt is made new.

But what is the new thing that the sacraments make? What is restored? What is brought back to life?

In the healing of the blind man, his sight is restored. What is restored to me via the sacraments?

There are probably several ways to answer this. I am saved from sin and restored to a state of holiness in the sacraments. My friendship with God is made new.

But probably the easiest way to describe what happens in the sacraments is simply to say that the love of God is brought to life within me. If I am remade by the sacraments, then I go from lacking God's love alive within me to having God's love alive in me.

In his first letter, Peter gives us a hint in this direction when he addresses his fellow baptized Christians, telling them that

baptism . . . now saves you, not as a removal of dirt from the body but as an appeal to God for a clear conscience, through the resurrection of Jesus Christ, who has gone into heaven and is at the right hand of God, with angels, authorities, and powers subject to him (1 Pet. 3:21–22).

In other words, baptism saves you because by undertaking it you appeal to God for a clear conscience, and Jesus, who "is at the right hand of God, with angels, authorities, and powers subject to him" has the power to make your appeal effective.

In baptism, you get a clear conscience—all of your sin and guilt are taken away.

But Peter goes on to describe in detail the new life of the Christian, imploring Christians to let go of old ways and take up new ways that are more consistent with baptism and the sacrifice of Jesus on the cross. He is emphatic in telling these Christians, "Above all hold unfailing your love for one another, since love covers a multitude of sins. Practice hospitality ungrudgingly to one another. As each has received a gift, employ it for one another" (1 Pet. 4:8–10).

Peter's description of love being "above all" for the baptized Christian gives us some confirmation that the sacraments are, primarily, about love.

Also, this understanding of the sacraments restoring love within us fits with the plain fact that Jesus makes love the primary theme of his preaching.

Nowhere is his desire to fill us with the love of God made more obvious than in the time before he is arrested to be tried and crucified. At that point, in the last moments he has to spend with his followers, he prays a long prayer for them that makes explicit his intentions in all that he does. He tells God the Father, "I made known to them thy name, and I will make it known, that the love with which thou hast loved me may be in them" (John 17:25–26).

Everything he has done and is about to do as he goes to the cross has been for this, "that the love with which thou hast loved me may be in them."

This one word, love, sums up both the moral and religious teaching of Jesus.

He is not just a moral teacher, he is the giver of a gift—divine love, and the moral life that he teaches flows from this gift.

The sacramental religion taught by Jesus is meant to remake us as creatures who have the love of God the Father alive within us. The moral life taught by Jesus is a life in which the love we have received is given—through acts of charity and mercy—to others.

Thus, if I ask what the sacraments restore in me, the simplest and most precise answer is divine love, which, in turn makes a life of love possible.

Love transforms life from hopelessness to hope, from bitterness to joy. It transforms suffering from meaningless to purposeful. This is why Jesus can teach that his yoke is "easy" but also teach that we must—yes—take up our cross each day and follow him.

It is easy to receive a sacrament and be remade. It is a joyful thing to be filled with God's love and to love others. But the life of love, though easy and light, is also profoundly difficult because it must be lived, for now, in a world that is not set up for love. To live as a person of love and mercy, forgiveness, and patience in a world that is full of brutality, carnality, and malice is to become vulnerable to insults and indignities.

It is like being a sheep among wolves. To live as a Christian, then, means that we face a daily choice between remaining in the love of God given by Jesus or abandoning it in the face of the hardships that, in this world, love inevitably brings.

In one of his most famous utterances, Jesus blesses those who do not surrender God's love or return to a worldly hardness of heart:

> Blessed are the poor in spirit, for theirs is the kingdom of heaven.
> Blessed are those who mourn, for they shall be comforted.
> Blessed are the meek, for they shall inherit the earth.
> Blessed are those who hunger and thirst for righteousness, for they shall be satisfied.
> Blessed are the merciful, for they shall obtain mercy.
> Blessed are the pure in heart, for they shall see God.
> Blessed are the peacemakers, for they shall be called sons of God.
> Blessed are those who are persecuted for righteousness' sake, for theirs is the kingdom of heaven.
> Blessed are you when men revile you and persecute you and utter all kinds of evil against you falsely on my account. Rejoice and be glad, for your reward is great in heaven (Matt. 5:3–12).

The love that is received in the sacraments that Jesus has given us transforms us from pride to poverty of spirit, from hard-hearted people to people who mourn the world's waywardness and suffering. This love enkindles in us a desire for righteousness and mercy, purity and peace. This is not a formula for avoiding suffering or the cross, but for wading into an often cruel and violent world with great vulnerability and compassion.

The person who lives this way shares, already, in the life of God, and so shares in all the sufferings the world heaps upon God's little ones. But by ending this litany of hardship and lowliness with the words, "Rejoice and be glad, for your reward is great in heaven," Jesus makes clear that the life of love has a horizon that the sinful life does not have. The life of lowliness has a richness that the life of pride misses. To have been remade by the love of God through the sacraments—and to have allowed that love to transform our manner of life into something like the life of Jesus—is to have become a citizen of heaven, one whose hope is not here but there; and that hope, Jesus says, will not be disappointed.

Jesus and Detachment

Jesus presents the fundamentals of his teaching in very simple terms. He begins his preaching with the words, "Repent and believe the good news."

The simplicity of this message is carried on by Peter and the other apostles in their preaching after the death and resurrection of Jesus. On the very first day the apostles went out to preach, Peter gave the people gathered in Jerusalem a long speech. He preached powerfully about Jesus, proclaiming him to be both "Lord and Messiah."

The people, deeply moved by the account of Jesus' suffering and death, asked Peter and the other apostles, "What are we to do, my brothers?" (Acts 2:37). In response to this very straightforward question, a question many ask today once they have been told about Jesus, Peter gives the basic instruction at the heart of his teaching: "Repent and be baptized, every one of you."

The simple action that Jesus and his apostles teach involves these two steps—detachment from the world (repenting), and attachment to God (believing in Jesus and being baptized in his name).

The detachment that Jesus teaches is not just a philosophical detachment—a meditation to help us avoid the sufferings of life. It is a move to get free of worldly desires so that we can have a true life of freedom to love God and neighbor.

Jesus illustrates this pattern of detachment and attachment time and again when he makes reference to himself. Whether in metaphors such as, "I am the vine, you are the branches" (John 15:5) or in bold literal declarations such as, "I am the way, the truth, and the life" (John 14:6), he makes clear that we must be attached to him in order to have the new life he is offering.

He even says, "Without me, you can do nothing" (John 15:5). Coming from anyone else this would seem like egotism, but from him it is an assertion of his divine power. He really is God, and we really do need to be attached to him in order to be what we were made to be—fully alive and free to love others generously.

The repentant person starts on a new path of life. Jesus describes this path when he teaches us to care for the poor, be unconcerned about possessions, forgive wrongs, and act with unreserved love for others. The baptized and believing person is made able to follow this path because God is made available to each person through the spiritual and religious practices Jesus instituted—such as being baptized, praying the Lord's prayer, sharing in communion, being anointed with holy oils, and confessing sins.

PART THREE

WHY PEOPLE STILL FOLLOW JESUS

19

The Pattern of the Christian Life

Almost everything we have talked about up to now happened in the distant past. So, even if it is all true, you might ask, "Why does it matter now? How is it connected to us, today, in the modern world? And in what way does it have any connection to me, personally?"

More than two billion people alive today say there is a connection, and here, in this last section of the book, we will try to understand why this is. Just what are such people talking about when they say that they are connected to Jesus now? When we know the answer to that, we will know why people still follow him.

The answer to this question begins with the belief that Jesus is risen from the dead. I can be friends with him here, and connected to him now, because he is risen from the dead—he is alive and present. But even knowing that Jesus is risen and alive does not answer the question about how he is connected to people today. It only answers the question about how it is possible.

The question before us in this last section of the book is not about how it is possible to be friends with Jesus. Rather, we are asking a more practical question: how does this friendship happen?

After all, if you asked me how I came to be friends with my wife, you would not find it acceptable if I answered, "Well, she is alive, and that is what makes our friendship possible." In fact, you would find such an answer to be weird.

It is not enough, then, just to point to the resurrection of Jesus as if that explained how people can be friends with him today. We need, rather, to explain the details, just as we would if you wanted to know about my relationship with my wife. How did you meet? How did you become friends and start dating? When did you know this was love? What is your life like together?

Knowing the answers to these questions would give you a sense of how our marriage came to be and what it is like.

But note that you would ask these particular questions because marriage is a particular kind of thing, and as such it has a pattern. My marriage is unique; there is no other like it in the world, but it is a marriage, and so it has certain features that it shares with every other marriage.

It will be helpful for us in this section of the book to know that this is also true of friendship with Jesus. Each friendship with Jesus is unique, but all friendships with him share certain features. There is, in other words, a pattern to friendship with Jesus.

I have had the privilege of participating in various forms of Catholic ministry over the last several decades, including my current work as host of *Catholic Answers Live*, one of the world's most widely listened-to Catholic radio programs. I have had the chance to speak to thousands of Christians both in person or on the air, and as I have discussed these things with many people over many years—people who often seemed very close to Jesus—the sense they conveyed about their encounters with Jesus was not that they discovered some new knowledge or came to an insight about something but rather that they knew, by means that many find difficult to describe, that he had intervened in their lives.

Many testify that at some point in their lives—maybe at a series of points over time—they came to have a sense (maybe faint, maybe sturdy) of Jesus' living presence.

This experience prompted them to take him seriously, and because they took him seriously, they attempted to pray as he instructed, to forgive others, to share with the poor, and to do the other things he commanded.

In doing these things, they found that encouragements flowered within themselves. It seemed to them that Jesus confirmed within them, either by outward signs or by inner movements, that he was indeed present.

As they prayed, they received clarity that felt as if Jesus had spoken, wordlessly, within their souls. This clarity was, for some, a correction that sent them in a new and more fruitful direction or, for others, simply an inner expression of love. Still others experienced a healing or the opening of a way that had seemed hopelessly closed—and this healing or opening contained a personal touch, something that confirmed for them that Jesus was present in the event. And some simply walked into a church or read the Bible and knew he was there, as happened in Notre Dame Cathedral to the great French poet Paul Claudel, who said, "In an instant, my heart was touched, and I believed."

Some of these people—far more, I think, than the world knows—have received powerful confirmations of Jesus' closeness to them. They have met him in dreams, heard his voice, witnessed miracles or other strange acts of divine power. Many have felt their own heart of stone turn to a heart of flesh in ways that surpass human explanations.

But these extraordinary experiences, though surprisingly common, are not shared by everyone who comes to friendship with Jesus, so I do not want to rely on them here in explaining the phenomenon of friendship with him. Rather, I am interested in describing the experiences common to all those many Christians who know that Jesus is alive and present because, in ways both simple and amazing, he has made himself known to them.

To explain the common pattern of the Christian life, I will take one exemplary Christian and look at the main features of the pattern of his life. Because his story is well known to almost every Christian, I have chosen Peter the apostle as our example.

Of course, for Peter, Jesus was a contemporary, a person walking this world just as anyone does. In this sense, Peter's experience of Jesus is unlike ours. But the writers of each of the four Gospels wrote for congregations full of people who had neither met Jesus nor lived with him as Peter had. And for new Christians who were following Jesus not because they had gotten to know him by the Sea of Galilee but because they had come to have faith in him, the Gospel writers present Peter as an obviously relatable figure, one who can be instructive for all Christians.

And what is more, the sheer volume of material related to Peter makes it possible for us to follow the full arc of his story—showing all the steps in his journey—in a way that we are not able to do for most of the other disciples.

Four moments, or stages, in Peter's relationship with Jesus stand out as universal:

1. Peter meets Jesus.

2. Peter's life is reoriented by following Jesus.

3. Peter shares in intimate friendship with Jesus.

4. Peter goes out to share Jesus with others.

In modern pastoral terms these moments, or stages, are often referred to as:

1. Encounter

2. Conversion

3. Communion

4. Mission

Let's look at Peter's first encounter with Jesus, at his conversion to Jesus, at his coming into communion with Jesus, and, finally, at the mission he undertook to share Jesus as widely as he could. This will give us a framework for understanding what happens to all those who come to follow Jesus today.

Jesus as God in History

Christians claim that, starting with Abraham and culminating in Jesus, God intervened in history. What is the evidence for this claim? Consider:

- The unique history of the Jewish people. This small shepherd people has survived for millennia despite constant attacks and despite constant pressure to assimilate. In the ancient world, they introduced entirely new ways of understanding the divine, and their claims about the oneness, justice, and mercy of God transformed the world. They have been just a sliver of the world's population, but it is impossible to imagine world history without them. All of this is evidence in favor of their claim to a special relationship with God.

- The unique influence of the Bible. How did an insignificant shepherd people come to assemble the most influential texts in human history? Why does this ancient book continue to influence individuals and world history as no other book does, even to this day? Its influence is evidence that something strange and wonderful is going on here.

- The strangeness of the person of Jesus as a unique teacher. He made unique claims about his own divine identity and, despite dying on a cross at thirty-three, he became the most influential person ever. After his death, his teaching made new modes of human flourishing possible, and his followers transformed the moral landscape of the entire planet.

We could extend a list such as this into a book of its own, but even these three facts demonstrate why it is reasonable to believe that God—through the Jewish people—has intervened in history. And it is even reasonable to believe, as those who witnessed Jesus raise a man from the dead exclaimed in Luke's Gospel, "God has visited his people!" (Luke 7:16).

20

Peter Meets Jesus

The first encounter between Jesus and Peter is presented to us in two different ways. Mark, Matthew, and Luke present Peter working as a fisherman in Galilee when Jesus calls him to become one of his followers. John, on the other hand, tells us that Jesus had gone out, like many people, to see John the Baptist in Judea, and that same time a group of men from Bethsaida, among Peter and his brother Andrew, also went to see John the Baptist. In this account, the Baptist testifies that Jesus is the "Lamb of God" (John 1:36) in front of Andrew, who begins to follow Jesus and who later introduces Peter to Jesus.

It is fair to surmise from the variations in the stories of how Peter and Jesus met that their meeting, like many meetings between people who later become friends, included starts and stops. People have overlapping circles of acquaintances, maybe they run into each other a few times, and, finally, they get to know one another. Something like this seems to have happened for Peter and Jesus. Clearly, none of the Gospel accounts of Peter's meeting with Jesus is a full account. Each Gospel writer gives a few details, the ones he thinks are important.

Perhaps it happened that Peter heard about Jesus from Andrew and from other people as well. At some point, at the time when Jesus was among those who went out to see John the Baptist, Peter was introduced to Jesus and Jesus impressed him. Jesus seems to have taken a particular interest in Peter as well, giving him a nickname early on. But Jesus did not immediately call Peter to follow him.

Mark's Gospel (followed, somewhat, by Matthew and Luke) relates an event that likely happened a little later, when Peter had returned to his work and home in Bethsaida near the Sea of Galilee. As Jesus began his preaching and healing ministry in the towns around the Sea of Galilee, he called Peter to follow him, and Peter—captivated by Jesus (and probably thinking by now that Jesus was, indeed, the Messiah)—followed.

One thing to note about the whole encounter between Jesus and Peter is that it is not presented to us as an encounter between an obvious sinner and his savior. Peter is not mired in sinful pursuits only to be rescued by Jesus.

I point this out because modern emotional accounts of Christianity often include the hopeless sinner who meets Jesus in a dramatic and salvific moment. Such stories do happen. But sometimes they are exaggerated for rhetorical effect, which can lead people who have ordinary encounters with Jesus, encounters similar to Peter's, to question whether they have really met Jesus at all.

Often, even in the modern world, one bumps into Jesus here and there before any friendship develops. There is not always a dramatic first moment. In Peter's case, lots of drama will come later as he follows Jesus, but their first meetings are piecemeal and modest. And even before he met Jesus, every indication we are given in the Gospels suggests that Peter was a solid Jewish man, living his faith as a responsible adult. He was not a decrepit sinner in desperate need.

So, if Peter is not yanked by Jesus out of the traps of sin, what, exactly, makes this encounter so special that Peter is willing to give up his usual life and become a follower? Answering this question is important because most Christians, despite the dramatic stories that some can tell, do not come to know Jesus in desperate circumstances.

Indeed, some people reject Jesus because they think they don't need him, because their lives are not at rock bottom. They think they are doing fine without him. Such people do not know what they are missing, and so they can easily let any encounter they might have pass by without responding to it.

Perhaps it looked like Peter was doing fine without him, too, in the usual ways of reckoning. But somehow Peter knew that he was not beyond needing Jesus, because he seems to have recognized in him the divine power that brings a human being fully to life. And doing fine and being fully alive are two very different things.

The power that Peter encounters in Jesus is something far beyond what human religious teachers and systems can provide. Even the daunting military power of the Roman occupiers is nothing compared to the raw and immediate power of Jesus.

Jesus says to a body, "Be healed," and it is healed. He says to a demon, "Come out," and it comes out. Water turns to wine at the merest direction from him. Everything—even the weather—obeys Jesus.

What is more, the power that Peter encounters in meeting Jesus is holy. It has not the slightest hint of selfishness but is placed entirely at the service of the sick, the possessed, the unlearned, the needy, and the unloved.

This, too, makes Jesus compelling. His fearsome power is meek and kind in its application. It is reminiscent not of the power of Pharaoh, but of Moses; not of earthly rulers, but of the prophets of old.

I do not want to suggest that sin and redemption play no part in Peter's story. Peter is a sinner whose sins are reported to us in the New Testament, and Jesus does, in fact, save him. But the entrance of Jesus into Peter's life is given to us in terms of God's stunning power, not Peter's change of heart. The power that Jesus displays as a teacher, a healer, and an exorcist—and the way Jesus uses this power to serve others rather than to exalt himself—fixes Peter's gaze on Jesus as the key. In the presence of Jesus, the-world-as-God-intends has become present within the sin-scarred world men have made for themselves.

In the presence of Jesus, some very basic questions about reality are definitively resolved.

Certainly, in the light of the actions of Jesus, Peter's Jewish faith is given irrefutable confirmation. The psalms that Peter has prayed all his life, and that Jews had sung for a thousand years, are proved true:

The LORD is faithful in all his words,
and gracious in all his deeds.
The LORD upholds all who are falling,
and raises up all who are bowed down.
The eyes of all look to thee,
and thou givest them their food in due season.
Thou openest thy hand,
thou satisfiest the desire of every living thing.
The LORD is just in all his ways,
and kind in all his doings.
The LORD is near to all who call upon him,
to all who call upon him in truth.
He fulfils the desire of all who fear him,
he also hears their cry, and saves them"
(Psalm 145:13–19).

And, at the same time that Peter's Jewish faith is affirmed, the deepest longings of his heart—those longings for fullness of truth, goodness, and beauty that are at the center of every human heart—are awakened. Many other things will happen in Peter's friendship with Jesus, but here, at the beginning, Peter is awakened to hope.

Is this real? Is this man truly the Messiah? Has the reign of God—filled as it is with healing and joy—finally come?

If the answer to these questions is "yes," as Peter suspects, then Jewish history is vindicated, the psalms are proven true, and the bright hopes of childhood are restored. All is well; life has meaning. The kingdom of God is not defeated, but here it is, right in the midst of what we were doing.

The awakening of hope, the experience of the world as new, the arousal of long-buried desire—these things are clearly only beginnings. But they bring a foretaste of what life can truly be when it is fully attached to the divine.

The general excitement as Jesus began going from town to town suggests that many people shared this experience with Peter. But how many went on to mature faith in Jesus? How many came to love him as Peter did?

We cannot know the answer to this, but certainly many did not. They delighted for a moment in the presence of Jesus and then returned to life as it had been. This should make clear to us that the encounter with Jesus guarantees nothing. In the encounter with Jesus, a new possibility opens, and that is all.

Many Christians, in fact, never move beyond this stage of relationship. Every Sunday as they sing and pray, they arouse themselves to feel again the newness of it, but they never move into real faith or abiding love. Many other people simply let the joy of encounter with Jesus fade as if it had never happened.

The encounter with Jesus is not a relationship with him. It involves no commitment, and it bears no fruit unless the hope and joy it arouses lead on to mature faith and love. But this doesn't mean that the moment of encounter with Jesus has no value. That would be like saying to a married couple that the moment of falling in love has no value because the real stuff of marriage and family comes later.

It is better to say that encounter is the crucial thing: the moment in which all possibilities open up and, in a certain sense, the wait is over. But this is true only if this moment leads on to the next thing and then the next.

So although this moment of encounter with Jesus does not guarantee that Peter will end up in the kingdom of God, without this encounter Peter would certainly remain outside it, toiling as a fisherman, waiting.

The encounter ends Peter's waiting and opens new paths, and no effort on Peter's part—no journey of discovery, no program of reform, no amount of study or meditation—could have brought this. Only the experience of the living God can do it.

Billions of Christians have had this experience. For them, the dawning of Jesus in their lives illuminated reality, answered fundamental questions, and brought to an end the time of waiting. Jesus came to them. They could not conjure or force or create this experience for themselves.

But to say that we cannot bring this experience about on our own is not to say that seeking after Jesus is pointless.

I have found, as I have listened to the conversion stories of other Christians, that many of them have made a harsh demand of Jesus: "If you are real and if you are God, make it so clear to me that I do not miss it." It astonishes me even to this day how many people report that such an approach worked. He made it so clear that they did not miss it.

And why not? The only thing that I am certain could stand in the way of such a prayer is bad faith. The person who is not really asking in good faith is not likely to recognize a divine response even when it comes.

But the person who asks to meet Jesus, so long as the request is made in good faith, will meet Jesus, without exception. Jesus says:

Ask, and it will be given you; seek, and you will find; knock, and it will be opened to you. For everyone who asks receives, and he who seeks finds, and to him who knocks it will be opened. Or what man of you, if his son asks him for bread, will give him a stone? Or if he asks for a fish, will give him a serpent? If you then, who are evil, know how to give good gifts to your children, how much more will your Father who is in heaven give good things to those who ask him! (Matt. 7:7–11).

What Did Jesus Found?

Jesus was many things—a teacher, a healer, an exorcist—but he was also the founder of an institution. In fact, he explicitly says that his intention is to found his own Church (Matt. 16:8). What was the Church that he founded to be like? Christians today do not agree on a single answer, which is why there are so many different types of Christian churches.

Despite the disagreements, one thing we can say for certain about Jesus' Church is that it was not meant to be a political or military power, in the sense of holding territory or forming an army. "My kingship is not of this world" (John 18:36), he said. He told people to give Caesar what belonged to Caesar and to give God what belongs to God.

Nonetheless, his institution was to have a lasting structure and a lasting task: to share the good news about him with the entire world.

The structure was simple. Jesus left his Church with a well-defined but small group of leaders to whom he gave the authority to act in his name, and he opened membership to everyone. This membership did not require much. He never asked that the members of his Church all live in one place or cease to participate in everyday life. Rather, they were to continue in the world but in a new way. All members were to treat one another as brothers and sisters, love others, have very high moral standards, and participate in the rites of the Church.

The leadership structure of his institution recalls the leadership structure established among the ancient Jews. For the Jews, the entire people were a "kingdom of priests" (Exodus 19:6), which is to say that the entire Jewish people had the role of drawing the world closer to God. But this priestly people also had a class of priests who served them and facilitated their relationship with God. And, finally, there was one high priest over the whole community.

The early Christians understood Jesus to be their one high priest, understood the apostles and those assigned by the apostles to be the priests for the community, and understood themselves, all together, to have taken on the role of God's priestly people.

Among them, this priestly function—the function of living in a covenant relationship with God and acting as his priestly people to bring God to the whole world—was no longer reserved only to Jews but could be shared by anyone who would accept baptism.

For them, baptism replaced the Jewish practice of circumcision, and all who were baptized became members of God's priestly people.

There was no other institution like it in the ancient world— one that welcomed anyone and existed for no other reason than to share news of God's actions so that people would come to God, love him, and love one another. This is what Jesus founded, a priestly community of the willing tasked with restoring all the world to friendship with God.

21

Becoming Like Him

Each day brought new encounters between Jesus and Peter. Each day, Peter got to know Jesus a bit more. And we can suppose, because such things happen when one friend reveres another, that Peter began to take on mannerisms and patterns of speech that he picked up from Jesus.

Also, as he listened to Jesus teach, the teachings had their effect. The words and acts of Jesus gave Peter a deeper understanding of the things of God and a greater determination to live as Jesus instructed.

Some of the change that happened in Peter was accomplished consciously: the disciple intentionally being mentored by the master and intentionally trying to imitate the master. Some of it happened unconsciously: the friend taking on more and more of the qualities of his friend.

But the sum of it was that each day, Peter's heart and mind began to take on the features of the heart and mind of Jesus.

The turning or conversion of Peter is the work of Jesus. He gives it content and by his life offers a perfect example.

But it cannot happen without Peter's willing cooperation. Conversion is a back-and-forth between teacher and student, a conversation between friends.

Everything Jesus does in their relationship is directed toward Peter's good; in cooperating with these intentions, Peter does his part. He counts his time with Jesus as more important than whatever else he had been doing, and day by day, building on his first encounter with Jesus and drawing new life from each new encounter with Jesus, Peter allows himself to be formed anew.

One might expect that this process of conversion would go very quickly, given who Jesus is. Clearly, Jesus is a perfect teacher and mentor, one who knows exactly what Peter needs at all times. And he is filled with divine power.

But Peter's conversion does not go quickly. In fact, his formation is remarkably slow. He does not change all at once, and sometimes he seems not to be changing at all. (This has been a great encouragement to Christians throughout history who find their own progress to be embarrassingly slow!)

It is notable that Peter's most famous failure does not come at the beginning of Jesus' ministry but at the end, after Peter has spent years following Jesus closely and being personally taught and formed by him. After all of that, and even after saying he would die with Jesus, Peter denies him three times.

It would be nice to think that seeing Jesus raised from the dead, and then receiving the Holy Spirit, would finally do the trick and complete Peter's conversion. But even as the leader of the early Church, Peter fails yet again (Gal. 2:11–14) and needs the somewhat bossy help of St. Paul to get back on the right track.

Conversion is not magic; it is the product of a relationship. And this seems to be exactly how Jesus wants it. For most of us, it seems, he would rather spend a lifetime working with us in patient interaction than circumvent the process with an instant transformation.

We can certainly imagine Jesus doing it in other ways. For example, he could have called Peter, and, having gotten Peter's permission, perfected him instantaneously by a miracle.

But Jesus does not do this for Peter. He lets the relationship do the work. In this way, Peter is made a partner to Jesus even in his own salvation. Jesus does not make him do it on his own; Peter does not have the power to reform and remake himself in order to share in the life of God. But in cooperation with Jesus, by step and by stumble, he is permitted the great dignity of participation in the work of his own transformation.

Jesus, it appears, does not will just that Peter be saved. He wills that Peter be saved in the manner that is most respectful of Peter's dignity as a creature of intellect and free will.

We saw an example of how Jesus works in Peter's life when Jesus called Matthew and his friends, opening up his inner circle to people Peter normally would have avoided. Whatever the discomforts of welcoming Matthew and his friends, Peter did not leave. And this is to Peter's credit. He remained and actively willed to prefer the way of Jesus to his own. In this way, a man who avoided sinners became one able to love sinners. And Jesus accomplished this transformation of Peter's heart not with a thunderbolt from heaven, like Zeus, but simply by sharing his life with Peter.

Throughout the Gospels, Peter shows an inspiring willingness to imitate Jesus and an impressive lack of caution in trusting him. These must have been among the qualities that endeared him so much to Jesus. They are certainly among the qualities that the Gospel writers wanted to commend to their readers.

Jesus walks on water, and Peter jumps out of the boat. Jesus says he is going to Jerusalem to die; Peter says he'll go die, too. That Peter often fails in his attempts to imitate Jesus is never counted against him. Though he sometimes corrects Peter, Jesus never stops helping Peter recover and continue in his formation.

In this way, they come to love each other as friends—the thing that Jesus most seems to want from all those who follow him.

Who Were the Apostles?

To the ancient Christians, the term *apostle* could refer to anyone with a mission on behalf of Jesus. But when we speak of the "twelve apostles," we speak about a special group of men chosen, trained, and commissioned by Jesus while he walked on earth. This group was given the role of serving the Church in imitation of Jesus by providing teaching, governance, exorcism, and healing.

At one point in his own ministry, Jesus "summoned the twelve and began to send them out two by two" (Mark 6:7). As they went out, the twelve imitated Jesus exactly, doing the same three things he always did in his ministry: "So they went off and preached repentance. They drove out many demons, and they anointed with oil many who were sick and cured them" (Mark 6:12–13). One of these apostles, Judas Iscariot, betrayed Jesus and then took his own life. His "office" as an apostle was then given to a man named Matthias, who had been among the disciples present for Jesus' entire public life.

For centuries thereafter, all Christians believed that the office of apostle was handed on to other men who came to be called bishops. Though not physical witnesses of Jesus' ministry, these bishops were assigned by the apostles to govern local church communities even during the years when the New Testament was still being written. (Two books of the Bible, First and Second Timothy, for example, are addressed to one of the early bishops of the Church.) After the Church splintered in the sixteenth century with the Protestant Reformation, not all Christians continued to recognize the office of bishop or retain direct succession from the apostles. But that office and that succession continue to this day.

The names of the apostles, in addition to Judas, are given in four places in the New Testament. They are Peter (aka Simon), John, James, Andrew, Philip, Thomas, Bartholomew (aka Nathaniel), Matthew (aka Levi), James son of Alphaeus, Simon the Zealot, and Judas son of James (aka Thaddaeus).

22

Intimate Friendship with Him

After he was raised from the dead, Jesus made time for a heart-to-heart talk with Peter, who had denied Jesus three times on the night Jesus was arrested.

Some of the disciples were out fishing on the Sea of Galilee. By a miracle, the risen Jesus filled their nets with fish, and:

When they got out on land, they saw a charcoal fire there, with fish lying on it, and bread. Jesus said to them, "Bring some of the fish that you have just caught." So Simon Peter went aboard and hauled the net ashore, full of large fish, a hundred and fifty-three of them; and although there were so many, the net was not torn. Jesus said to them, "Come and have breakfast." Now none of the disciples dared ask him, "Who are you?" They knew it was the Lord. Jesus came and took the bread and gave it to them, and so with the fish. This was now the third time that Jesus was revealed to the disciples after he was raised from the dead.

When they had finished breakfast, Jesus said to Simon Peter, "Simon, son of John, do you love me more than these?" He said to him, "Yes, Lord; you know that I love you." He said to him, "Feed my lambs." A second time he said to him, "Simon, son of John, do you love me?" He said to him, "Yes, Lord; you know that I love you." He said to him, "Tend my sheep." He said to him the third time, "Simon, son of John, do you love me?" Peter was grieved because he said to him the third time, "Do you love me?" And he said to him, "Lord, you know everything; you know that I love you." Jesus said to him, "Feed my sheep. Truly, truly, I say to you, when you were young, you girded yourself and walked where you would; but when you are old, you will stretch out your hands, and another will gird you and carry you where you do not wish to go." (This he said to show by what death he was to glorify God.) And after this he said to him, "Follow me."

Peter turned and saw following them the disciple whom Jesus loved, who had lain close to his breast at the supper and had said, "Lord, who is it that is going to betray you?" When Peter saw him, he said to Jesus, "Lord, what about this man?" Jesus said to him, "If it is my will that he remain until I come, what is that to you? Follow me!" (John 21:9–22).

On one level, this is a straightforward story about a rough patch in the relationship between Peter and Jesus. On this level, it is a tale of failure and reconciliation. Peter has blown it by denying Jesus three times, which almost certainly has left in Peter's heart a residue of anxiety that resurfaces as he faces the risen Jesus. And by asking Peter to confess his love not one or two or four but three times, Jesus is clearly acknowledging the rupture in their relationship—and trying to move Peter past it.

This we might call the lowest level of meaning. It is specific to Peter and Jesus. It is between the two of them. Peter's personal shame needs to be addressed, and Jesus does so with kindness by asking Peter to do privately what he had failed to do publicly.

Related to this personal level of meaning, but on a higher and more public level, this story is about Peter's role in the Church.

Peter is to lead the Church that Jesus is founding. And this story clearly contains profound teaching about the kind of leadership Jesus is asking for. The Church does not need a leader who is his own man, so to speak, but one who is a man for Jesus.

Jesus makes clear that leadership of the Church must flow from a personal love for Jesus: "Do you love me . . . feed my sheep." Both of these levels of meaning are specific to Peter: one involves Peter the man who has sinned, and the other involves Peter in his role as the leader of the Church.

But between the private relief of Peter's personal shame and the public bestowal of Church leadership, there is a level to this story that is really meant as a message for every Christian. On this middle level, the story of Peter's conversation with Jesus is a story about the very meaning of each Christian life.

At its root and at its height, Christian life is friendship with Jesus—a friendship so close that it is called communion. This story is about the kind of communion Jesus is offering.

Probably the easiest way to consider what Christians mean by communion is to consider the example of marriage. All marriages are communities, but not all marriages are communions. When they join themselves to one another, spouses enter a new community. This community has visible features—a public ceremony of union, the private intimacy of the marriage bed, the sharing of property, home, and possibly children. And all of this is good.

If this is all that a marriage ever is, it is a very productive community.

But in some marriages, the spouses come to share in something deeper. They come to be friends who know and are known, who love and are loved. And this friendship becomes a shared life of love, one in which they find abiding joy.

In this communion, each spouse lives, in a sense, for the other. Each wills the happiness of the other and enjoys the happiness of the other. Such participation in the life of another makes life different. It exposes the truth that life, in its fullness, is shared. There is no fully human life that is not shared.

Certainly, we do not have to be married to another person to enjoy communion with him or her. Friendships, sibling relationships, monastic relationships, and many other kinds of relationships are capable of becoming shared lives of love.

Communion with others is life's greatest joy because it satisfies the deep desire of the heart to "be with" rather than to merely "be." And communion with Jesus is the greatest possible instance of life's greatest joy because he alone can satisfy the desire not just to "be with" another, but the ultimate desire of every heart to "be with" God. In Jesus, God has come to be with each of us, as the name Emmanuel ("God with us") foretold (Isa. 7:14, Matt. 1:23).

God does not remain remote; he does not invite Peter into a pseudo-communion that is purely transcendent, as if God were a dazzling light that Peter could simply choose to approach or retreat from. In Jesus, the transcendent God has come down.

This is the reason Jesus has been born, why God has taken on the life of a man: so that Peter (and anyone who meets Jesus) can enter into an intimate, two-way friendship with God.

Humanity, for millennia, has searched for God, built temples, ziggurats, and pyramids, created intricate religions with magnificent ceremonies. Men have sacrificed dogs and cats, doves and cattle, captives from war, and even their own children in their efforts to transcend the limits of this world and break on through to the other side. Men have taken potions, sweated in lodges, fasted, prayed, inebriated themselves, and denied themselves in every way.

Many of these efforts have been undertaken in good faith; others have been steeped in darkness and injustice. But always the goal was to transcend this world and go up to the divine. This need for transcendence is more or less the difference between a human being and every other kind of being on earth. And always the assumption is that some great distance—whether physical or spiritual—must be traversed to achieve this transcendence and to encounter the divine.

But what if the divine wants to break on through to this side, wants to come down right in our midst where it's easy to find him?

This is the opposite of religion as humans have always practiced it. Rather than taking place on an exotic plane or requiring stringent practices and arduous quests, in Jesus' religion God shows up in the midst of the ordinary and seeks ordinary friends. The communion Jesus offers is companionable: a charcoal fire, a simple meal, friends gathered by the sea. He intends to treat us as brothers and sisters; to be not just our master but our friend.

To achieve such communion—the communion of true friends—involves persons breaking down masks and illusions that separate them. Here, Peter has failed and is vulnerable, and this allows Jesus to open himself to Peter with radical frankness. Peter's illusions about himself have been shaken, and this provides an opening through which Jesus' voice can be heard inviting Peter, at his very depths, to come out of himself and into a shared life. Peter does not have to go up Olympus, as a pagan hero might, in order to come face to face with God. He just has to let down his guard. To let himself be befriended.

In this conversation with Peter by the lake, we see Jesus in a state of perfect openness. His question about whether Peter loves him is not just a test for Peter, but it is a revelation of himself to Peter as one who truly wants Peter's love.

Jesus, in this moment, is like the boy who asks the girl, "Do you want to dance?"

In asking this question he takes a great risk because he reveals himself as wanting to dance with her. He uncovers his heart and leaves it up to her whether or not to crush it.

Jesus calls out to Peter, "Do you love me?" These are not the words of someone who only wants to fix Peter or set him on firm ground to lead the Church. These are the words of one who is revealing his own heart and calling out to the heart of the other.

And Peter is right when he says, "Lord, you know I love you." Jesus does already know the answer. So, why does Jesus keep asking?

In one sense, he keeps asking because he wants to be utterly unmasked. In this moment when Peter's own failure still stings, he makes himself utterly open to Peter.

The words *follow me* give us a powerful clue about what Jesus is doing. They hearken back to something Jesus said earlier in John's Gospel: "My sheep hear my voice, and I know them, and they follow me" (John 10:27).

The theme of shepherding is so strong in this passage that Jesus makes it impossible for us to miss it. Each time he asks about love, he acts as a shepherd who is leading Peter toward meeting him where he wants to be met. He wants Peter with him as a shepherd wants his sheep secure within the pasture. The "pasture" toward which the Good Shepherd leads his flock is abiding friendship with himself.

Here, before he leaves his disciples for the last time, he is shepherding Peter into this pasture by revealing his own heart, the heart of one who truly wants the love of friendship with those he has made his brothers and sisters.

Communion with God, it turns out, is more than just living in God's presence, more even than loving him and being loved by him. Both of these are unimaginably good things, but neither quite captures the dear friendship God is offering to each human in the person of Jesus: a love as if of equals, a friendship in which neither party is at a disadvantage and in which both parties are at ease.

To explore the full depths of what Jesus is offering here, we must take a moment to go back to Peter's betrayal of Jesus and consider exactly what it is that Peter has done wrong.

We must ask, "In what way, exactly, did Peter fail?"

It is clear that Peter did not fail to do something that Jesus had asked him to do. Jesus never asked Peter to come die with him in Jerusalem. Jesus never asked Peter to put himself in any peril at all.

In fact, Jesus tried to shake Peter free of such thoughts. Consider the context in which Peter promised to die with Jesus, in John chapter thirteen. The Last Supper has concluded. Jesus has washed the disciples' feet and, in a state that the Gospel writer describes as "deeply troubled," Jesus has predicted that Judas is about to betray him. He has spoken profoundly to them about his love for them. He has called them his friends. And now he is predicting his own death by saying, "Where I am going, you cannot follow me now, though you will follow later."

Peter's response to all of this badly misses the mark. What Peter says to Jesus in this moment is, in fact, deeply hurtful.

Peter said to him, "Lord, why cannot I follow you now? I will lay down my life for you." Jesus answered, "Will you lay down your life for me? Truly, truly, I say to you, the cock will not crow, till you have denied me three times" (John 13:31–38).

Peter neither comforts Jesus nor praises him, nor shows any sign of gratitude or friendly concern. In this moment of impending torture and death for Jesus, Peter chooses bravado.

And with his response to Peter, Jesus stings: "Will you lay down your life for me?" Such a question suggests that Jesus is trying to pierce a layer of unreality. Peter is engaged in his own drama. He is trying to be the hero of his own story, but he is not the hero. He is the one being saved.

Peter's death will add nothing to what Jesus is about to do. Peter's place in this drama is purely receptive. He must allow Jesus to do this for him. Jesus is the one whose death restores the friendship between God and man. A man, such as Peter, must simply accept the restored friendship as a gift, as something he could not gain for himself.

So, later, when Jesus meets Peter on the beach, the ritualistic repetition of the words "Do you love me" represents a re-do for Peter, in which Jesus reveals to us what he really wanted from Peter as he went to his death.

It is as if Jesus is telling Peter, "When I so wanted just to hear that you loved me, you got caught up in your own drama. The only response I wanted to my love was your love. Let us go through this little ritual so that you can let go of your failed heroics, let go of thinking that I ever wanted heroics from you, and return to our friendship."

The proper response to Jesus offering himself on the cross, it turns out, is not, "I will die, too." It is simply, "I love you."

The fact that Jesus refers to Peter by his full name, "Simon, son of John," adds to the sense that he is trying to break through to Peter. The formality of it, the repetition of the name three times, all gives a sense that Jesus is calling Peter to attention, to wake up and be aware of what is really going on here.

And when this whole ritual of healing and awakening is over, Jesus predicts Peter's death and says, "Follow me."

Peter, who had promised to die heroically for Jesus, will, in fact, die for Jesus. But this will not be a heroic death like that of a pagan hero. Rather, it will be like Jesus' death, not glorious but quiet, seemingly senseless, yet offered out of love of others and for the building up of the kingdom of God.

Note that Peter never stops referring to Jesus as "Lord" throughout this exchange, and Jesus doesn't ask him to. That is what should shock us about this entire exchange—the Lord, the creator of all, is here as a man trying to get Peter to let go of whatever else he thinks he is doing and just be his friend.

He is the God/man, and he can have no equal, but he chooses to give himself in friendship, a relationship of equals. His friendship is filled with power and grace, and it elevates the other person to a kind of equality in which each can accept the other as friend. Each can offer what he has and be accepted by the other.

Nothing, absolutely nothing—no heroics, no feats of physical or spiritual effort, not even faith—is an adequate response to the friendship given by Jesus. Only love, to love him and accept his love, is an adequate response.

After Jesus predicts Peter's death and says, "Follow me," Peter does, in fact, get up and follow him. The two of them walk away from the others. This moment alone with Peter gives this entire exchange its definitive meaning. This is the moment when, having restored Peter to friendship and confirmed him not as a servant but a collaborator (one who does what Jesus does), Jesus can walk with him as a friend.

Whatever hardships will come, Jesus is Peter's friend, and Peter has learned simply to return the friendship of the Lord. The two of them walk side by side along the sea.

What Is Jesus Doing Now?

At the end of Mark's Gospel, Jesus leaves his disciples and ascends into heaven. But the same Gospel immediately makes clear that he did not truly leave them:

> So then the Lord Jesus, after he had spoken to them, was taken up into heaven, and sat down at the right hand of God. And they went forth and preached everywhere, while the Lord worked with them and confirmed the message by the signs that attended it (Mark 16:19–20).

His return to heaven, in this understanding, means that he takes up the throne of the king—"sat down at the right hand of God." But as the king, he continues to help the disciples to carry out the mission he has given them: "The Lord worked with them."

The end of Matthew's Gospel includes a promise to be with them as they accomplish the mission he has given them: "Go therefore and make disciples of all nations, baptizing them in the name of the Father and of the Son and of the Holy Spirit, teaching them to observe all that I have commanded you; and lo, I am with you always, to the close of the age" (Matt. 28:19–20).

His physical departure from the earth is not an abandonment of his followers but seems instead to be an empowerment. He has taken up the role of king over heaven and earth, and he has delegated to those he loves the job of spreading news of his kingship.

23

Sharing Him with Others

Jesus is not here with us in the same way he was with Peter by the Sea of Galilee. He ascended into heaven and will return at some future time, in glory. But he has left us what we need in order to have communion with him. He has left us a living Church that offers us his words and his sacraments.

And, just as his communion with Peter ("You know I love you Lord") makes Peter a collaborator in the work of Jesus ("Feed my sheep"), we are meant to infer that our communion with Jesus also makes us collaborators in his work.

The stages that Peter has gone through—meeting Jesus, changing to become like Jesus, and sharing in the communion of friendship with Jesus—open out onto the world. Peter spends the last thirty years of his life sharing Jesus out of love, in the hope that others will receive what he has received: communion with the living God.

Those who encounter Peter—because Peter is in such intimate communion with Jesus—also encounter Jesus.

And this begins the pattern of the Christian life for them.

They might ignore what they encounter in Peter and go on without considering it. They might become initially excited by the introduction to Jesus that Peter brings, but then lose interest and go back to what they were doing. Or, they might go on, as Peter did, to become an intimate friend of the God who became a man.

Having met Jesus through Peter, they can follow Peter, learn from him, and become more and more like Jesus. Through the sacramental life of the Church, they can have spiritual and physical contact with Jesus and enter into the communion of friendship with him. And then, because they have such intimate communion with Jesus, others can meet Jesus through them.

In this way, it turns out that the missionary work of Peter and the other apostles, a mission that called others into the communion of love offered by Jesus, was brought to me. People down through the centuries kept meeting him, learning to be like him, entering into the communion of friendship with him, and introducing other people to him until, eventually, some of those people became my parents and teachers, my pastors and friends, and through them I was introduced to the Bible, the sacraments, and Jesus himself.

I came to know him as alive by two means: others shared him with me through words and actions, and he shared himself with me, directly and inwardly, by communication with my soul.

I do not think it is in any way a spiritual brag to say this second thing. I have known hundreds, thousands, of fellow Christians who say quite openly that Jesus has communicated directly with them through voices or visions (though this is rare), through spiritual experiences, or through signs and miracles. As I have said, this is far more common than many people realize. For me, these communications are not voices or images, but something else.

I dreamed once that I was in a dark ocean, and beneath me I could feel a whale moving. The whale moved its massive body with terrifying power. I rose and fell on the water as the great creature slid and rolled below.

In the dream I never saw the whale or felt its touch, but I knew it was there and that it was aware of me.

The wordless, awesome (and possibly playful?) communication of the whale's presence that I experienced in that dream, a communication that is below what can be seen or heard, struck me when I awoke as an image of what it is like to know Jesus.

When he moves, my little life moves, even if I do not feel his physical touch. Though I never hear a word, I know he is there in awesome (and possibly playful?) power.

The medium through which I experienced the whale was water. In relation to Jesus, the medium is meaning. Internal experiences of the soul have meaning, and that meaning rolls out into the heart and mind, sometimes with great clarity as if words were spoken, sometimes only as an intimation of love, an assurance of the presence of the beloved.

I learned (very, very slowly and reluctantly) to become like him, and, one day, I understood that I was living in a communion with him. He to whom I can never be equal had called me into the equality of friendship. Though it took a very long time, I learned to stop whatever else I was doing and simply return his love, to love him as my friend.

He speaks to me, though I have never physically heard a word from him. He loves me and is kind to me. He never gives up on me. He fills me with joy and gives me power I never imagined that I would have—power to overcome sin, to forgive from my heart, to bring peace and healing, and to share a life of communion with others.

Everything is different with him.

Though I have none of her mystical experiences, I know that Jesus says to me just what he said to Julian of Norwich: "All shall be well, and all shall be well, and all manner of thing shall be well." He says it every moment, and, bit by bit, I surrender and truly believe him. In those moments when I do, everything is different because of the peace he gives.

Jesus is the Son of God come down in love.

He teaches a morality of love and equips his disciples (primarily through sacraments of love) to love others on his behalf.

People meet him all the time, and those who are willing to be sent he sends out into the world to bring the kingdom of God to others:

Repent, and be baptized
every one of you

in the name of Jesus Christ
for the forgiveness of your sins;
and you shall receive the gift of the Holy Spirit
(Acts 2:38).

About the Author

Cy Kellett is the host of the popular radio program *Catholic Answers Live*. He formerly hosted *The Bright Side with Cy Kellett* on the Immaculate Heart Radio network. For more than a decade Kellett was editor of San Diego's diocesan newspaper, *The Southern Cross*. Before that, he taught high school and then spent several years working with the homeless mentally ill in Massachusetts while living in a Catholic Worker house. Cy and his wife, Missy, have three children. *A Teacher of Strange Things* is his first nonfiction book.